The Bible is GOD's Word!

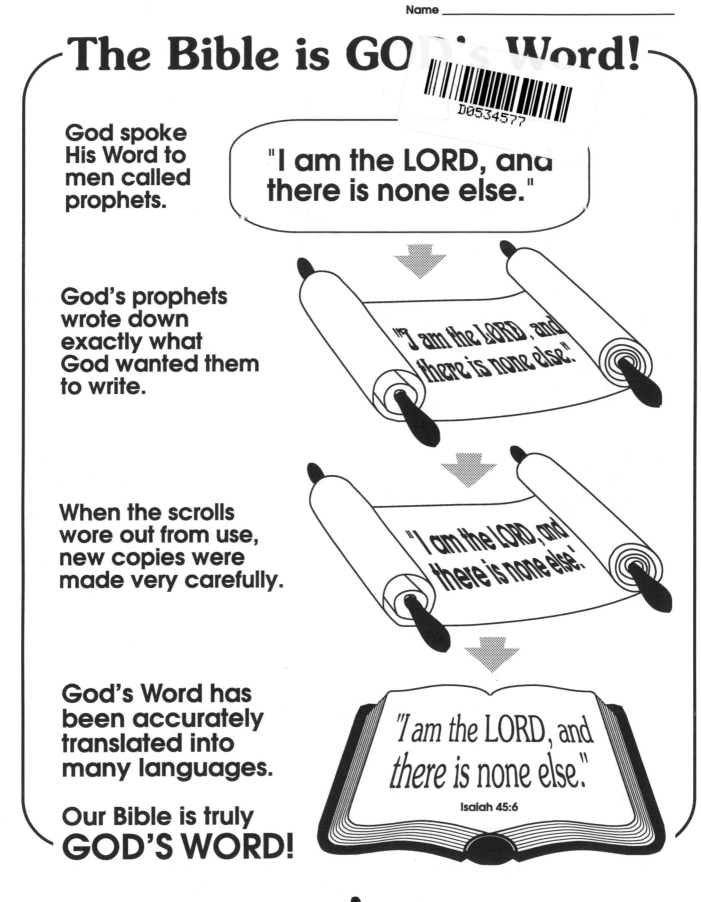

God spoke His Word to men called prophets.

"I am the LORD, and there is none else."

God's prophets wrote down exactly what God wanted them to write.

"I am the LORD, and there is none else."

When the scrolls wore out from use, new copies were made very carefully.

"I am the LORD, and there is none else."

God's Word has been accurately translated into many languages.

"I am the LORD, and there is none else."

Isaiah 45:6

Our Bible is truly **GOD'S WORD!**

Introducing the Bible

Readers: Uncle Don, Travis, Jessica

Uncle Don:
Hi, Jessica. Hi, Travis. What are you doing today?

Travis:
We're bored.

Jessica:
Mom said we could come over and visit you for a minute if we don't bother you.

Uncle Don:
You're not a bother. I'm glad to have you. It's not every uncle that has his niece and nephew right next door! I'm glad you moved here—especially since your dad is travelling so much now.

Travis:
I like coming over here to see you.

Jessica:
I know you! You like the cookies and milk he gives us!

Travis:
You're right!

Uncle Don:
I just happen to have some more cookies. I'll get some for us.

Travis:
Uncle Don, what were you reading?

Jessica:
That's his Bible. Don't you know? He reads his Bible a lot—don't you, Uncle Don.

Uncle Don:
Yes, Jessica, I do. It's the greatest of all books.

Travis:
What's so great about it?

Uncle Don:
It's God's book—God is the author of the Bible.

Travis:
Do you mean that He wrote it?

Uncle Don:
He had men write down His Words. The Bible is God's personal message to each one of us.

Jessica:
To us? I thought it was written a long time ago.

Uncle Don:
It was. Actually, God used over 40 men to write down all His Words. And it was written over a period of 1,600 years.

Travis:
1,600 years? You must be kidding!

Uncle Don:
No, God had men write down His messages for years and years until everything was written down that He wanted to tell us. The Bible is the greatest and most accurate of all history books. But better than that, the Bible is God's story.

Jessica:
You mean it is about Him?

Uncle Don:
Yes, Jessica, God is the One whom the Bible is all about. It's not just history; it's HIS STORY!

Travis:
The Bible is an awfully big book. I don't know how anyone could ever read it all.

Uncle Don:
You'd be surprised. I've read it through many times, and each time I enjoy it more and want to read it more.

Travis:
You mean you've actually read that whole big book lots of times? Why?

Uncle Don:
Travis, the Bible has the answers for all the important questions of life. The Bible never changes, because God never changes. Everything He had written down thousands of years ago is still useful to us today.

Jessica:
You mean it's not just a bunch of old stories?

Uncle Don:
Absolutely not. Everything recorded in the Bible is true. And everything recorded there is for us to know. God wants us to know Him.

Travis:
You mean, like we know a person?

Uncle Don:
Yes, only God is greater than anyone. You really **can** get to know Him. How would you kids like to start to learn about God?

Jessica:
I'd like to.

Travis:
Me, too.

Uncle Don:
First we'll need to check with your mom, to make sure it's okay with her. Then we can set up a time to meet and study the Bible together. I think you'll be surprised how much you will learn and how much sense it will make to you.

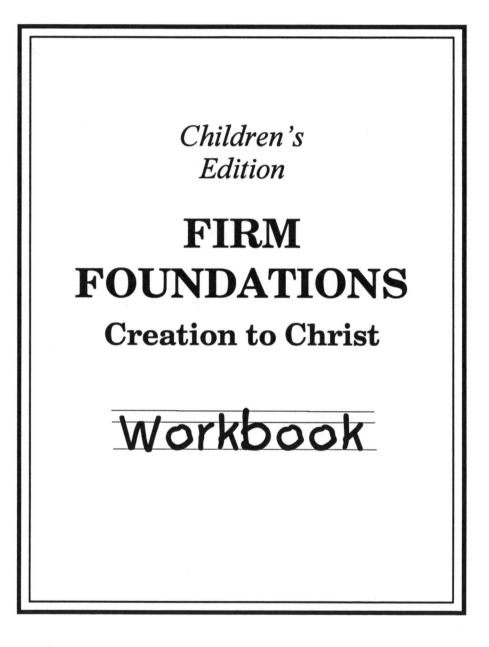

Children's Edition

FIRM FOUNDATIONS

Creation to Christ

Workbook

New Tribes Mission, Sanford, FL 32771-1487

Name _____

The Bible is the Word of God

Write out II Timothy 3:16 and memorize it.

_____

_____

_____

_____

_____

_____

Use this WORD BANK to fill in the blanks to the questions below. Cross out each word on the list as you use it so you can see what is left.

WORD BANK: God   1,600   Jewish   40   communicates   prophets

---

1. When God wanted His words written down, He chose men to write them. He put into their minds the exact words He wanted written. These men who wrote down God's Word are called

   _____.

2. These men lived at different times and in different places. As a matter of fact, it took about

   _____ years before all of God's Word was written down.

3. God used about _____ men to write His Word.

4. All but one of them were of the same nationality—they were _____. (Luke was a Gentile—not a Jew.)

5. Who is the author of the Bible? _____

6. The Bible is God's personal message to every one of us! God _____

   with us! He tells us what we need to know.

skit 2

God Alone

Readers: Uncle Don, Travis, Jessica

Travis:
Guess what, Uncle Don! We're going to go camping next weekend!

Jessica:
You should see all the stuff we're taking.

Travis:
I even got a new flashlight!

Jessica:
And I got a sleeping bag!

Travis:
I already had one for scouts.

Jessica:
There are three families going from where Mom works. Everybody is bringing part of the food. All Mom has to bring is desserts.

Travis:
I hope she brings a lot!

Jessica:
Oh, Travis! You're **always** hungry!

Uncle Don:
Where are you going?

Travis:
Up to the lake.

Uncle Don:
That's a beautiful place. But you sure do have to bring in everything you'll need. There's nothing up there but the trees and the water—no stores or houses.

Jessica:
I never realized how much stuff we do need!

Uncle Don:
You're right, Jessica. We really do need a lot just to live. Of course, most of us have more than we really need. Did you ever stop to think that God doesn't need **anything**?

Jessica:
What do you mean, Uncle Don?

Uncle Don:
Just exactly that—God doesn't need anything. God has always been and always will be. He existed before anything was created. He was there before there was any light or air or food or water; He existed before the angels!

Travis:
But didn't God have a beginning sometime?

Uncle Don:
No, God is eternal—He had no beginning and He will have no end.

Travis:
How can that be?

Uncle Don:
God is greater than our understanding. God is greater than all! The very first words in the Bible are "In the beginning, God . . . ."

Jessica:
So He was there in the beginning?

Uncle Don:
God was there **before** the beginning.

Travis:
But where did He come from?

Uncle Don:
That's the exciting part, Travis. Everything else had a beginning. **God had no beginning.** He simply **IS**, eternally. And He doesn't need **anything**.

Jessica:
Doesn't he need people?

Uncle Don:
No, Jessica. There was a time when nothing existed but God. No air, no light, no people—nothing but God.

Travis:
Wasn't God lonely?

Uncle Don:
No, God is very, very special. The Bible tells us that he is really three persons in one. We call God a "Trinity." We can't begin to understand how wonderful He is. God the Father, God the Son, and God the Holy Spirit—who are together the One great God—have existed forever.

Travis:
Now I am confused.

Uncle Don:
You know, Travis, I don't even **try** to understand some things about God—I just accept them by faith. He is so much greater than anyone can ever imagine! God is not like us. But we **can** know a lot about Him, just by studying His Word, the Bible. God is truly wonderful, and **He wants us to know Him!**

Jessica:
Mom said that Travis and I could study the Bible with you.

Uncle Don:
Yes, I talked with her, too. I'm eager to start. Let's start right here at the beginning, with that verse I told you about in Genesis 1:1.

 **man**

GOD is the greatest! Use the words in the shaded column to finish the sentences below. One word in each block goes with the description of God, the other word goes with the description of man.

God had no beginning and will have no end. God is _____ .	**dies** **eternal**	Man is born and _____ .
God is a _____ ; He is three persons in One.	**Trinity** **one**	Man is only _____ person.
God needs _____ .	**nothing** **many things**	Man needs _____ _____: food, air, water, sleep, light, etc.
God is _____ ; He does not have a material body.	**body** **spirit**	Man has a material _____ .
God is _____ , all the time.	**one** **everywhere**	Man can only be in _____ place at a time.
God is _____ than all and more important than all; He is the highest authority.	**greater** **authority**	Man should be under God's _____ and listen to everything God says.
God was there _____ the be-ginning of everything.	**not** **before**	Man was _____ there before the beginning.

Travis:
That was a scary movie last night.

Jessica:
Mom told you not to watch it.

Travis:
I know. But part of it was exciting. I didn't want to turn it off. Oh, hi, Uncle Don.

Uncle Don:
Hi, kids. What was exciting?

Travis:
Oh, Nothing.

Jessica:
A movie he watched last night. Mom told him not to, but he went back and watched it anyway while Mom was gone for a while.

Uncle Don:
Travis, did you disobey your mom?

Travis:
Yes, I did. I know it was wrong. I wanted to see this movie. Part of it was neat, but part of it was really scary. It was all about these evil spirits and then there were these good spirits.

Uncle Don:
Travis, you really need to obey your mother. You need to go and apologize to her, if you haven't already. And your mother is right—that was **not** a good movie.

Travis:
I've seen other movies like that, Uncle Don. And some of the kids at school see them all the time.

Uncle Don:
Travis, the problem is that movies like that don't show the truth. They are designed to get your attention and make you want to keep watching, but there's nothing good in them—only evil.

Travis:
But are the spirits real? Where did the devil come from?

Jessica:
Travis, you shouldn't ask that!

Uncle Don:
It's all right to ask that, Jessica. As a matter of fact, I was going to suggest that we see what the Bible says in answer to those very questions.

Travis:
The Bible?

Uncle Don:
Yes, the Bible. That's the place to find the truth. Those movies will only put lies into your mind. But God's Word will show you what is true and good. Did you know that the Bible tells us that all the spirit beings, called angels, were originally created by God?

Jessica:
You're kidding!

Uncle Don:
No, in the beginning, God created everything. All of the angels were created by God to be His servants. They were all created **perfect!** God created so many angels that it would be impossible to number them.

Travis:
And all of them were good?

Uncle Don:
All of them were **perfect.** God made the angels very strong. They were created to be His servants and messengers. He gave some of the angels special skills and special jobs to do. The greatest of all the angels was called Lucifer. God put Lucifer in charge of the other angels.

Travis:
Lucifer—isn't he really Satan? Do you mean he was a good angel at one time?

Uncle Don:
That's right. He was created perfect by God. But after a while Lucifer became very proud of his great beauty, intelligence, and his position over the other angels. He decided he wanted to be like God—he wanted to be like the Most High. Lucifer became the very first one to do evil.

Jessica:
That's terrible!

Uncle Don:
Yes, it really was. And some of the other angels followed Lucifer in his rebellion against God.

Travis:
I didn't know this was in the Bible.

Uncle Don:
God did not let Lucifer and his followers get away with their rebellion. God is greater than all.

Jessica:
What did God do?

Uncle Don:
He removed them from their positions of service in Heaven—and He prepared a terrible place of everlasting punishment for them.

Travis:
God really is strong!

GOD created the angels

Find the hidden message! Put the answers to the questions in the numbered spaces of the puzzle, using the **WORD BANK.** Then fill in the rest of the blank spaces between the heavy lines to tell how great God is!

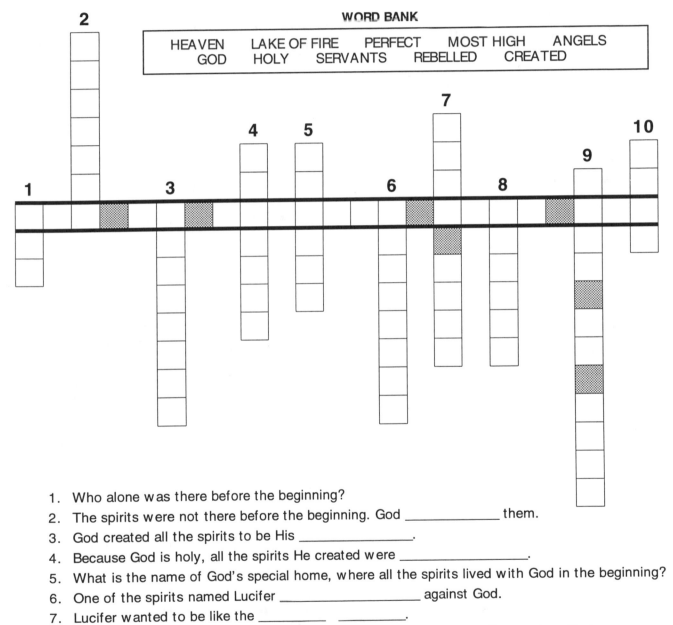

WORD BANK

HEAVEN	LAKE OF FIRE	PERFECT	MOST HIGH	ANGELS
GOD	HOLY	SERVANTS	REBELLED	CREATED

1. Who alone was there before the beginning?
2. The spirits were not there before the beginning. God _____ them.
3. God created all the spirits to be His _____.
4. Because God is holy, all the spirits He created were _____.
5. What is the name of God's special home, where all the spirits lived with God in the beginning?
6. One of the spirits named Lucifer _____ against God.
7. Lucifer wanted to be like the _____ _____.
8. Many of the other _____ also followed Lucifer in his rebellion against God.
9. What is the name of the place where one day, God will cast Lucifer and all his followers?
10. God has never sinned and never will sin. He will not allow those who sin against Him to stay in His presence. God is sinless and perfect. In other words, He is _____.

LESSON 4 **FIRM FOUNDATIONS REVIEW SHEET**

Uncle Don:
Hi, kids!

Jessica and Travis:
Hi, Uncle Don!

Travis:
I'm glad you could come early!

Uncle Don:
Actually, the clock is wrong—I'm a couple of minutes late. The power was off this afternoon for an hour and a half. You kids must have been outside when the lights went off.

Jessica:
You're right. We were out playing.

Uncle Don:
Travis, weren't you planning to finish your science project today?

Travis:
Well, I wanted to, but I haven't gotten all the things I need to finish it. I didn't realize how many materials I'd need.

Uncle Don:
What are you making?

Travis:
Oh, it's just a model of the world.

Uncle Don:
Just a model of the world? That sounds pretty complicated to me. How are you making it?

Travis:
I'm using some clay stuff and wire and . . .

Jessica:
He's really making a mess.

Travis:
She's right, I'm making a mess.

Uncle Don:
You've gotten into a pretty big project, Travis. Do you know how the world really was made?

Travis:
I don't know. Does anybody know for sure?

Uncle Don:
Yes, and we can **all** know for sure, because the One who made it had someone write down how He did it.

Jessica:
Where is it written?

Uncle Don:
It's written in the Bible. God, who created all the spirit beings, also created the earth. He was the only one there in the beginning, and He knew exactly what happened.

Travis:
Well, how did God do it?

Uncle Don:
The Bible says that God **created** the heavens and the earth. He simply **spoke** and there was light.

Travis:
Wait a minute—what did He use to make the earth?

Jessica:
Where did the light come from?

Uncle Don:
The Bible tells us that God made everything from **nothing**.

Travis:
But how could God do that?

Uncle Don:
God is all-powerful; nothing is impossible to Him.

Travis:
But aren't there a lot of people who don't believe that?

Uncle Don:
Yes, Travis, there are. They are some of the same people who can't get their work done when the power goes out and who can't get their jobs done when materials aren't available. But God is never lacking anything. You know, when you were outside, you didn't even know that the power went off. The light there didn't even flicker.

Jessica:
Do any of the scientists believe the Bible?

Uncle Don:
They certainly do, Jessica. The Bible has the only sensible explanation for everything that we see in the world. And God's record of Creation in the Bible never has changed and never will, either. The more that scientists study the Bible, the more they have to realize that every word of the Bible is true.

Travis:
I think my science project is too much for me to handle. Uncle Don, will you teach me more about what the Bible says about Creation?

Uncle Don:
Travis, I'll be glad to! Maybe we can find something for your science project, too. The Bible is the best place of all to learn!

Name _____

GOD
Created
EVERYTHING

1. Genesis means _____.

2. God created everything out of _____.

3. God could create everything because He is _____.

4. God knows _____.

5. Who was there before the beginning? God the _____, God the _____, and

   God the _____ _____.

6. On the first day, God _____ and there was light.

7. On the second day, God placed some of the _____ from the world high up

   above the sky.

In your Bible, look up Hebrews 11:3.
Write the verse on the lines below.
When you have memorized it, try to
write it from memory on the back of
this sheet.

**CIRCLE THE
RIGHT ANSWER:**

GENESIS is the   last
                       middle   **book of the Bible.**
                       first

_____

_____

_____

_____

Travis:
Look, Jessica! They're coming up!

Jessica:
What's coming up?

Travis:
The seeds I planted for my latest science project—look at them!

Jessica:
You're right, Travis, they are! How many kinds do you have?

Travis:
Well, there are four: two kinds of vegetables and two kinds of flowers. I couldn't believe all the different kinds of seeds Uncle Don showed me.

Jessica:
Where did you go?

Travis:
We went to the garden shop. They had racks just full of all different kinds!

Jessica:
The thing that gets me is that every one of those little seeds can make a plant. They look all dried up but you put them in the soil and add some water and there comes the plant!

Travis:
I know. I'd never really thought about it until Uncle Don showed us. I really liked all the things he showed us under the magnifying glass, too. Jessica, please hand me that packet of petunia seeds.

Jessica:
Oops! I spilled them. What a mess. They went everywhere. Oh, hi, Uncle Don.

Uncle Don:
It looks like Travis is getting some help on his science project.

Travis:
Jessica is making a mess!

Jessica:
These are hard to pick up. They're so tiny!

Uncle Don:
Tell me, Jessica, did they fall into a nice, neat pattern?

Jessica:
No, they went everywhere. I can't even find most of them.

Uncle Don:
It looks like Travis was able to get some seeds in the right place. Your seedling boxes look nice and neat. Look at this little row of green sprouts!

Travis:
I'm really excited! This was a great idea!

Uncle Don:
Kids, do you realize that all these seeds had their origin from plants that God created in the beginning?

Jessica:
I never thought about that!

Uncle Don:
God is the creator of everything.

Travis:
My science teacher says that everything happened by chance. He says that all the different kinds of things just "evolved" over the years.

Uncle Don:
Travis, did you notice what happened to the seeds Jessica dropped?

Travis:
They went everywhere.

Uncle Don:
How about the seeds you carefully planted?

Travis:
They're right here, in a row.

Uncle Don:
What made the difference?

Travis:
She's messy and I'm neat.

Jessica:
Travis! I didn't mean to drop them. They just happened to fall.

Uncle Don:
You could say that they just fell there by chance, couldn't you. But Travis decided exactly where he would put his seeds, and they are in a nice row. What do you think? Do you think that all the patterns in flowers and trees and leaves and animals happened by chance?

Jessica:
They couldn't! That would be impossible. Somebody had to make them that way!

Uncle Don:
That's exactly right, Jessica. God did. He is the designer of everything.

Travis:
I never knew there was so much to learn in the Bible. And this is just from the first chapter!

God created everything

DESIGNER

CREATOR

God designed everything

This picture shows many things which God created and designed. List the things you can find!

_____
_____
_____
_____
_____
_____
_____

Use this WORD BANK to fill in the answers to the questions below:
God   spoke   God   loves   designer   good

1. God created many varieties of plants and trees and flowers because He _____ us.

2. To create the sun, the moon, and all the stars, God just _____ .

3. All of the laws that control the universe were originally established by _____ .

4. Can anyone besides God make a living creature?   YES   NO

5. God said that everything He created was _____ .

6. Whenever you see a design, you know that there had to be a _____ .

7. Who designed everything in the universe? _____

Have you learned Hebrews 11:3? Try to write it out from memory. Look in your Bible to see if you are correct. When you have this verse memorized, write it again on the back of this paper.

_____
_____
_____
_____
_____

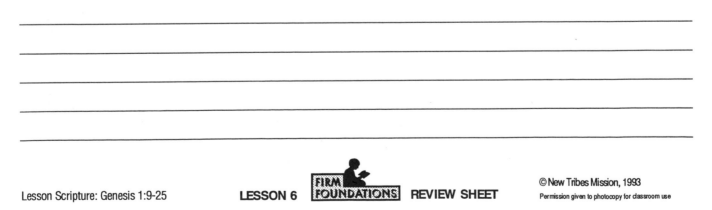

God Created Man

Readers: Uncle Don, Travis, Jessica

Uncle Don:
Hi, Jessica. It's good to see your dad home from his business trip.

Jessica:
I'm glad he's home. We miss him when he's gone so much.

Uncle Don:
Well, he misses you, too. Where's Travis?

Jessica:
Oh, he's over in the garage talking to dad about that wooden chest he found in the moving stuff.

Uncle Don:
Travis sure wanted that! He was trying to convince himself that it was just some moving box. But I know that your dad made that himself. I don't remember all the details, but I think it has a special purpose.

Jessica:
Here comes Travis now.

Uncle Don:
Hi, Travis. How are you today?

Travis:
Fine, thanks. Uncle Don, I'm sure glad I listened to you and waited for dad before I took that wooden chest and put my model stuff in it!

Uncle Don:
Well, I knew that your dad had made it himself, and I think it has some special purpose.

Travis:
He did make it! I couldn't believe it! It's really neat. He said he doesn't have time to do that kind of work now that he travels so much.

Jessica:
So what's it for, anyway?

Travis:
It holds all of his antique woodworking tools. He said he's had them packed away for years. When we moved he decided that he was going to put them out on display in that case again. He made the case when he and mom were first married.

Jessica:
It's beautiful! Where did he get the tools?

Travis:
They belonged to his great grandfather. Every space in that case holds one of those tools just perfectly!

Jessica:
I'm glad you didn't put your models in it!

Travis:
Me, too! Dad said he might make me a case someday—just special for my models. I'd sure like that!

Uncle Don:
There's a good lesson in that wooden case.

Jessica:
What do you mean?

Uncle Don:
Well, your dad made that case. He owned it, and it was his to do with as he pleased because he made it. He designed it for a special purpose. Did you ever stop to think that God made man?

Jessica:
Made man? Out of what?

Uncle Don:
The Bible tells us that God made man out of the dust of the ground.

Travis:
Dust? Our science book says man just evolved.

Uncle Don:
The Bible tells us that God made the first man out of the dust. And it was God who breathed life into man. God is the Creator of man, the owner of man. Man belongs to God. God is the one who knows what man is made for, and the one who knows what is best for man.

Jessica:
I never thought about that!

Uncle Don:
Most people don't. But it's very important. Your dad made that wooden case, therefore it belonged to him. He made it. It was up to him what should be done with it.

Travis:
And here I was trying to believe that it was just a moving box and I could do whatever I wanted with it!

Uncle Don:
Travis, that's kind of like the way people think when they refuse to believe that God created them.

Travis:
What do you mean?

Uncle Don:
People who think that man evolved don't realize that God is the Creator and owner of man. They think they can do whatever they want.

Travis:
Just like I almost did with the case!

GOD CREATED MAN IN HIS IMAGE

GOD CREATED MAN IN HIS IMAGE

> **Use the words in this WORD BANK to fill in the answer to the questions below. Cross out each word you use so you can see what words have not been used. The finished sentences will tell you a great deal about God and how much He loves man!**
>
> love   Adam   in His image   belongs   man   know   obey   earth

1. God prepared the earth for _____ .

2. The great difference between the creation of the animals and the creation of man is that God created man _____ _____ _____ .

3. God gave man a mind so man could _____ God; God gave man emotions so man could _____ God; God gave man a will so he could _____ God.

4. Who is our very first forefather? _____

5. After God created Adam, the first man, God gave Adam control over the _____ and everything in it.

6. God could give the earth to man because God made the earth and everything _____ to Him.

On the lines below, write out Genesis 1:27 and memorize it. Then see if you can write this verse from memory on the back of this sheet.

_____

_____

_____

_____

_____

God Placed Adam in Eden

Readers: Uncle Don, Travis, Jessica

Travis:
Guess what! Dad is going to build me a case for my models!

Uncle Don:
That's great! I heard he was going to have an extra week before his next business trip.

Travis:
Guess what else! He's going to teach me some woodworking stuff. He said I might even get to put the finish on the case!

Jessica:
Oh Travis, you're too messy to do that.

Travis:
No, I'm not!

Uncle Don:
Kids! Your dad will probably show you a good way to do it so it won't be quite such a messy job. He really knows how to work with wood.

Travis:
And he's going to teach me to use the handsaw and the electric drill and the sander and some other tools, too. But he won't let me use the power saw.

Jessica:
You'd probably cut yourself.

Travis:
No, I wouldn't!

Jessica:
Yes, you would!

Uncle Don:
Jessica, Travis—that's enough!

Travis:
You should see all the tools he's got. I never knew he had so many. And he knows how to use every one of them. And he's going to teach me!

Jessica:
Well, you're not the only one who gets to do something special. Mom said she and I could bake cookies together for you and Dad!

Uncle Don:
That's great. Your dad and mom really love you and Travis. I know they're glad to have some time to spend with you.

Jessica:
I just wish Dad were home more.

Uncle Don:
So does he. But his job requires him to travel almost all the time.

Travis:
Maybe he'll change his mind about the saw. I'd really like to use that saw. Just think of all the things I could make!

Uncle Don:
Travis, you are going to get yourself into trouble. Your dad made it very clear he doesn't want you using that saw.

Travis:
I know. But it looks like so much fun!

Uncle Don:
Travis, don't you understand? Your dad made that rule **because he loves you**. He knows that you aren't old enough yet to control that saw. It's a very, very dangerous piece of equipment.

Travis:
I think I could handle it!

Uncle Don:
And your dad knows you **couldn't** handle it! Look at all the things he's going to help you learn to do. Why don't you just enjoy those and quit fussing about the saw?

Jessica:
He likes to fuss.

Travis:
So do you.

Jessica:
I do not! Mom won't let me change the oven racks, and I listen to her. I don't want to get burned.

Uncle Don:
Jessica, you're right about obeying your mom, but you do fuss sometimes, don't you!

Jessica:
Well, sometimes.

Uncle Don:
Your parents love you and provide for you and teach you, and they make rules for you because they know what is best for you. I think this would be a good time to look at our Bible story in Genesis. You will see in the Bible that God had that kind of concern for Adam.

Travis:
Do you mean that Adam had to obey God?

Uncle Don:
God did not **make** Adam obey—but He told Adam what was **good** to do and what he **must not do** and **what would happen** if he disobeyed—just like your dad does with you.

GOD Placed Adam in Eden

Unscramble the letters to find the words to fill in the blanks.

God always does all He plans to do. God always does what He says. God never _____.
HAGNECS

God rested on the seventh day because all His work of creating was _____.
FDSIHENI

In the beginning, all the plants were watered by a mist or streams from the ground; there was no _____.
NARI

God placed Adam in Eden. He did not ask Adam; He just put Adam in the garden. God could do this because God _____ Adam. Adam rightfully _____ to God.
TEARCDE **GDELEBON**

Because God created everything and every person, _____ in the world really belongs to God.
YNGERVEHTI

God placed two special trees in the middle of the garden: the tree of life and the tree of knowledge of good and evil.

God told Adam he could eat from all of the trees in the garden except one. In the sentence at the left, find the name of that tree and circle it.

God said that if Adam disobeyed God and ate from the fruit of the tree of knowledge of good and evil, Adam would surely _____. The penalty for sin is death:
EDI
1. Immediately, Adam would be separated from God.

2. Eventually, Adam's body would die.

3. Finally, Adam would be cast into the Lake of Fire, separated from God forever.

Write out Psalm 24:1, 2 and memorize it.

_____

_____

_____

_____

Travis:
This cold is miserable.

Jessica:
I think I'm catching it, too.

Uncle Don:
I've had one myself for about a week now. Kids, did you know that in the beginning there was no sickness?

Travis:
That would be great! You could keep on playing outside no matter what the weather was like!

Uncle Don:
In the beginning, the weather was perfect, too. As a matter of fact, **everything** was perfect. And it was perfect because **God is perfect**, and He created everything perfect and good.

Jessica:
Was Adam perfect, too?

Uncle Don:
Yes, Jessica, he was, because God created him perfect. Adam didn't even have to work hard to keep the garden—there weren't any weeds growing.

Travis:
Adam must have been happy!

Uncle Don:
Yes, I think he was. God knew exactly what Adam needed. And He knew that Adam needed a companion, so God made Eve.

Jessica:
Did he make her out of the dust, too?

Uncle Don:
No, the Bible tells us here in Genesis that God put Adam to sleep and removed one of Adam's ribs. From that rib, God made the first woman.

Travis:
How did God do that?

Uncle Don:
God knows how to to everything. He is all powerful and he knows everything! Now Adam would not have to be alone. Eve was God's gift to Adam.

Jessica:
You mean God made her just for Adam?

Uncle Don:
That's right—God made Eve to be the perfect helper for Adam.

Jessica:
Were they married?

Uncle Don:
Yes, Jessica, they were. That was God's perfect plan for Adam and Eve. He told them to become just like one person.

Travis:
You mean they were not supposed to be separate any more?

Uncle Don:
That's right, Travis.

Travis:
Did they argue with each other?

Uncle Don:
Not in the beginning. They had perfect friendship with each other and with God. As a matter of fact, God came and talked with them in the garden.

Jessica:
I wonder what the garden was like?

Uncle Don:
It must have been wonderful! Imagine all of the flowers and vegetables and trees and fruits and berries—all the colors and fragrances and sounds and good things to eat—what a place!

Travis:
Did Adam and Eve have to do anything?

Uncle Don:
God gave them the most important job on earth—to be the rulers over everything He had made.

Jessica:
He gave all that to them to take care of?

Uncle Don:
Yes, He did. God made everything for man and He wanted to help them take care of it all.

Travis:
I'd sure like to have seen that garden!

Jessica:
Me, too!

Uncle Don:
Yes, it must have been more beautiful than we could ever imagine—well, it was **perfect**, because God is perfect!

Travis:
Uncle Don, the Bible sure tells it better than my science book!

Uncle Don:
The Bible tells the **true story of creation**—God's story. God wants us to know the truth!

Name _____

GOD Made Eve

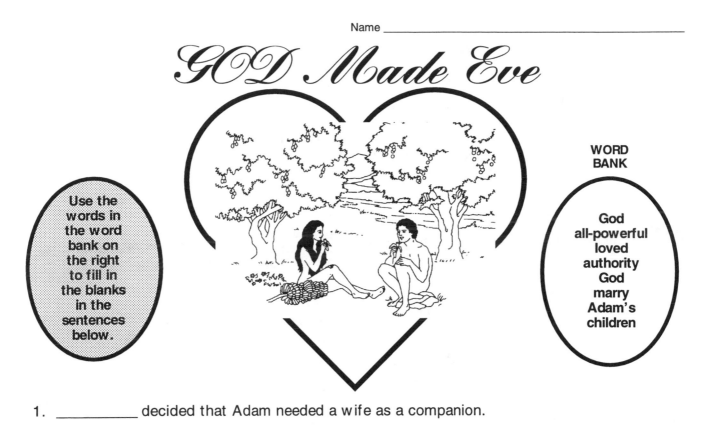

Use the words in the word bank on the right to fill in the blanks in the sentences below.

WORD BANK

God
all-powerful
loved
authority
God
marry
Adam's
children

1. _____ decided that Adam needed a wife as a companion.

2. God decided to make a wife for Adam because God _____ Adam and did not think it was good for Adam to be alone.

3. It was right for God to make a wife for Adam without asking Adam first, because God is the final _____ over every person and everything.

4. God made the first woman from one of _____ ribs.

5. God was able to make Eve from one of Adam's ribs, because nothing is impossible for God. He is _____-_____.

6. God told Adam and Eve to _____ and have _____.

7. At this time, marriage was good and happy because Adam and Eve were living just the way _____ told them to live.

Can you write out Genesis 1:27 from memory? Look in your Bible if you need help.

_____

_____

_____

_____

Lesson Scripture: Genesis 2:18-25   LESSON 9 FIRM FOUNDATIONS REVIEW SHEET   © New Tribes Mission, 1993
Permission given to photocopy for classroom use

Jessica:
Uncle Don, I'm sure glad we moved next door to you!

Travis:
Me, too!

Uncle Don:
I'm really glad too! It's a lot of fun to get to know you kids. If you hadn't moved here, we would hardly know each other right now.

Jessica:
That's right! We didn't live that far away before, but we never got together.

Travis:
Now we see you just about every day.

Uncle Don:
And I love it!

Travis:
I never knew you knew so much about gardening. Would you believe it—that science project you helped me with—I got an A!

Uncle Don:
You did the work. I'm glad you enjoyed it. I've learned a lot about you, too—Jessica loves to bake cookies and Travis loves to eat cookies!

Travis:
You're right!

Jessica:
I brought some! Do you want some now?

Uncle Don:
That's great, Jessica! Thank you. We can have some before we have our lesson.

Jessica:
That's another thing I learned about you—I didn't know you liked to read so much. You are always reading your Bible!

Uncle Don:
You know, Jessica, it's just like our visits. We've learned about each other because we are spending time together. Like you said, we used to live fairly close, but we never got together.

Travis:
But now we're seeing each other and learning a lot about each other! May I have a cookie?

Uncle Don:
Sure, Travis. Jessica, these are good. I'll bet you and your mom have a good time baking together.

Jessica:
I love it! Mom is a lot of fun.

Uncle Don:
And you really enjoyed working on that wood project with your dad, didn't you, Travis.

Travis:
That was great! I didn't realize all the things my dad could do! I just kept watching him and watching him. He's really good with tools.

Uncle Don:
You know, you kids have been learning a lot, being with your parents and watching them work. I think you might be surprised how much you are learning about someone else, too.

Jessica:
Who is that?

Uncle Don:
Well, I was thinking about God!

Travis:
God?

Uncle Don:
Yes! We've been reading about the things God did in creating everything. I think we've already learned quite a bit about Him. Let's see—what do you know about where God is?

Travis:
He's everywhere—all the time!

Uncle Don:
Very good! How great is He?

Jessica:
He's the greatest! No one is as great as God!

Uncle Don:
You are right, Jessica. God is greater than all. Was there ever a time when God was not living?

Travis:
No, He's always been alive.

Jessica:
He always will be! He's eternal!

Uncle Don:
What does God need in order to exist?

Jessica:
He doesn't need anything!

Uncle Don:
What did God use to make everything?

Travis:
He didn't use anything! He just spoke! You know what? We **are** learning a lot about God!

Uncle Don:
Yes, you are. God is **wonderful** and there's so much more to learn about Him!

Name _____

Greater than all!

Perfect, Holy

ALL-POWERFUL

GOD

IS

Everywhere, all the time

ALL-KNOWING   **LOVE**   **UN-CHANGING**

The **CREATOR** of ALL

LESSON 10    FIRM FOUNDATIONS   REVIEW SHEET

Travis:
Was that ever stupid!

Jessica:
What, Travis?

Travis:
A kid in my class—he got himself expelled from school today.

Uncle Don:
Do you know what happened?

Travis:
Sort of. This kid is always doing dumb stuff. And he steals things sometimes. This time he got caught stealing a tape recorder from the principal's office. Now that is stupid!

Jessica:
Will he have to go to jail?

Travis:
I don't know. I just know he was stupid to do something like that. Anybody would know that's wrong and you can get in big trouble for doing it. He said, "The devil made me do it."

Jessica:
That's **really** stupid! Who would want to follow the devil?

Travis:
Not me!

Jessica:
Me neither!

Uncle Don:
Would you be surprised if I told you that most people who follow the devil didn't really plan to?

Travis:
What do you mean?

Uncle Don:
Satan is very clever. He is totally evil. But he usually disguises himself so that people don't even recognize him.

Jessica:
But isn't everything about him bad?

Uncle Don:
Yes, it is, but he often makes himself appear very good so people are fooled.

Travis:
I don't think he'd fool me.

Uncle Don:
You'd better not speak so quickly, Travis. Satan's very name means deceiver, or tricker.

Jessica:
You mean he plays bad tricks?

Uncle Don:
He certainly does. I want you kids to know what God says about Satan in the Bible. We're going to study Genesis 3 which tells how Satan came to Adam and Eve.

Travis:
You mean he came into the garden?

Uncle Don:
Yes, Travis, he did.

Travis:
I got a book from the library and it says that the story in the Bible about Adam and Eve is just a myth.

Uncle Don:
Travis, that book you got at the library is a very good example of how Satan works to trick or deceive people.

Travis:
But this is a nice book. It has lots of good stuff in it.

Uncle Don:
It may appear that way. But what is written in it is really saying that God is a liar.

Jessica:
A liar! God doesn't lie!

Uncle Don:
No, He doesn't. But this book is saying that the story of Adam and Eve is not really true—it is just a myth. God tells us in many places in His Word that the story of Adam and Eve is true. Who do you suppose is right? God or that library book?

Travis:
I didn't realize, Uncle Don! I was almost tricked into believing that library book just because it looked so good.

Uncle Don:
Travis, there's another danger here. The boy at school said that the devil "made" him do it. I think the story in Genesis 3 will make you think about that statement. People not only are tricked into disobeying God; they also **willfully disobey** Him.

Jessica:
You mean, they do bad things because they want to?

Uncle Don:
I'm afraid so. That's what happened to Adam. 📖

Name _____

Adam and Eve Disobeyed GOD

1. When Satan came to deceive Eve, did he let her know who was talking to her?   YES   NO

2. God told Adam that, if they ate the fruit from the tree of the knowledge of good and evil, they would surely die. But Satan told Eve they would not. What was Satan suggesting God to be? ____ _____.

3. Does Satan still try to trick us today?   YES   NO

4. God said that Adam and Eve would die if they ate of the fruit of the tree of the knowledge of good and evil. Satan said they would not die. Who spoke the truth? _____

5. Adam and Eve did not fall dead immediately when they ate of the fruit of the tree of knowledge of good and evil. God had said that they would die for their disobedience. He meant that:

   They would be _____ from God, their friend and source of life.

   Their _____ would eventually die.

   They would eventually be separated from God forever in the _____ ____ _____.

6. When Adam and Eve realized they were naked, they made clothes of fig leaves for themselves. They should have asked _____ for help instead.

7. What did Adam and Eve do when they heard God coming to see them? They _____ .

Use this WORD BANK to fill in the answers to the questions above:
bodies   God   a liar   Lake of Fire   hid   God   separated

Knowing God: God is always true. He loves us.

Knowing the Enemy: Satan is a liar and a deceiver. He hates God and man.

God's Promise and Curse

Readers: Uncle Don, Travis, Jessica

Jessica:
Did you hear what happened to Travis yesterday?

Travis:
Jessica!

Uncle Don:
It's all right, Travis, your mom called me and told me about it. How is your hand?

Travis:
It hurts—a lot.

Uncle Don:
You are really bandaged up! I don't think you'll forget that experience for as long as you live.

Travis:
I'd like to.

Uncle Don:
Yes, I imagine you would. I'm glad your dad was there to help you. I thought he wasn't coming back until today. He must have surprised you.

Jessica:
Their meetings were over a day early and he flew back yesterday afternoon.

Travis:
It was awful. I had just turned on the saw. I was going to make a neat present for Dad. Then Jessica hollered at me and scared me. It was her fault!

Jessica:
Travis! It was **your** fault! You disobeyed Dad!

Travis:
I don't think the saw is made right. You shouldn't be able to cut yourself on it.

Uncle Don:
Are you sure it wasn't **my** fault?

Travis:
What do you mean? Oh, I guess I **am** blaming everyone else. It **was** my fault. Anyway, when Jessica hollered, I bumped the saw blade with my hand. It was awful! Somehow, I got the saw turned off. And just then Dad drove up.

Uncle Don:
What did you do, Travis?

Travis:
I didn't know what to do. I tried to hide, but I was bleeding too much. Dad just wrapped a towel around my hand and took me right to the hospital. It was scary.

Jessica:
Mom and I were scared, too. We had to wait so long for Dad to call from the hospital to tell us you were okay!

Uncle Don:
What did the doctor tell you?

Travis:
Well, he said it was really bad. He said I nearly lost the use of my thumb, and I may always have problems with it.

Uncle Don:
Travis, do you realize what happened?

Travis:
What do you mean?

Uncle Don:
Do you realize that your disobedience nearly cost you part of the use of your hand?

Jessica:
It could have killed him.

Uncle Don:
Yes, if someone hadn't been there to help you, you could have bled to death. Travis, I hate to see that you've been hurt so badly, but maybe it will help you see the seriousness of sin. That's just what we're going to study about in Genesis. There are consequences to sin, and I'm afraid you are facing some of them.

Jessica:
That's what Dad told him when they got home.

Travis:
You know something? I was so afraid that Dad was going to be mad at me. But he didn't say hardly anything on the way to the hospital. He just kept looking over at me and asking me if I was doing all right.

Uncle Don:
Your Dad loves you, Travis.

Travis:
I know. He promised to teach me to use the saw one day, when I get older. He did bawl me out when we got home, but he did something I've never seen him do. He and mom cried.

Jessica:
We all cried.

Uncle Don:
Travis, sin affects everyone. We're going to read about Adam and Eve, and I want you to see how they acted and how God responded to their sin. I think that you will identify a little with what happened. And God made a promise, too— a wonderful promise for sinners.

Name _____

GOD's Promise and Curse

1. After Adam and Eve had sinned, God called to them because He wanted them to _____ their sin.

GOD SEES
SIN

2. Can anyone hide from God?   YES   NO

3. God had the right to question Adam because God _____ Adam. Adam belonged to God.

4. God promised to send a Deliverer who would overcome _____ and deliver men from death.

5. God promised to send a Deliverer because God _____ people.

6. Did Adam and Eve deserve God's love and His promise to send a Deliverer?   YES   NO

7. Who were the first parents of all people? _____ and _____

8. All people _____ because Adam, the first man, disobeyed God.

Use this WORD BANK to fill in the answers to the questions above.
loves   Adam and Eve   admit   Satan   created   sin

ACREG ____ ____ ____ ____ ____

Unscramble the letters to find the word that means

GOD'S UNDESERVED KINDNESS

VELIDRERE

____ ____ ____ ____ ____ ____ ____ ____ ____

Unscramble the letters to find the word that means

SOMEONE WHO RESCUES, SAVES US

On the back of this paper, write out Hebrews 4:13 and then memorize it.

MAN'S SIN BROUGHT GOD'S CURSE.

In the beginning, God created everything perfect and good. But when man **sinned,** all of God's creation suffered from the curse.

Pain. sickness, death, hard work, sorrow, separation, fear, destruction, disease, violent weather, all started as the result of man's _____.

Lesson Scripture: Genesis 3:9-20

FIRM FOUNDATIONS

LESSON 12   **REVIEW SHEET**

Uncle Don:
How is your hand doing, Travis?

Travis:
It still hurts a lot. But I think it's a little better.

Jessica:
It would be better if he didn't keep banging it.

Travis:
I know. But it's hard not to. I keep trying to do stuff for myself, but I just can't do it. It's embarrassing. I even need help getting dressed.

Uncle Don:
I can sympathize with you. I hurt my hand real badly once. But it's a good reminder that there are some things we really can't do for ourselves. We need help.

Jessica:
Like what?

Uncle Don:
Well, there are lots of things we need help with, but I was thinking particularly of our sin problem. God won't accept anything we try to do ourselves to take care of our sins.

Jessica:
Doesn't the Bible say, "God helps those who help themselves?"

Uncle Don:
No, that's something man thought of. It's not found anywhere in the Bible.

Travis:
It's hard not to be able to help yourself. I'm tired of it. I can't do anything with this big bandage.

Uncle Don:
We really like to do things ourselves, don't we?

Travis:
Dad said he did something almost like I did when he was just a little boy.

Jessica:
He did? What did he do?

Travis:
Well, he disobeyed his dad, just like I did.

Jessica:
Disobeyed? Dad disobeyed his dad?

Travis:
He did! He was told not to use this big axe they had for chopping firewood.

Jessica:
What happened?

Travis:
He used it anyway. He said he thought he was getting pretty good at splitting wood when he missed and hit his foot.

Jessica:
Oh, how awful!

Travis:
It was awful. He said that's why he limps a little now. I never thought about it before. He showed me the scar. It must have been really bad.

Jessica:
I just can't imagine Dad disobeying!

Travis:
I can!

Uncle Don:
Kids, I think you need to understand something. We are all sinners. We were born sinners.

Jessica:
Born sinners?

Uncle Don:
Yes, born sinners. We have inherited a lot of things from our parents, and they inherited a lot of things from their parents (your grandparents), and so on. We inherit our hair color, our eye color, our height, and lots of other things.

Travis:
But what's that got to do with being born a sinner?

Uncle Don:
Travis, do you remember what we said about everyone being related to Adam?

Travis:
Adam and Eve were the first parents of all people.

Uncle Don:
That's right. And because Adam sinned, his sin was passed on to his children and to their children and right on down to us. Everyone is born a sinner because we are descendants of Adam who sinned.

Jessica:
That's not fair!

Uncle Don:
Jessica, man rebelled against his Creator. Sin affected **everything** in all creation.

Jessica:
Can't we do something about it?

Uncle Don:
No, there's nothing we can do. Only God can help us.

Name _____

GOD's Provision and Judgment

Circle the correct answers to the YES and NO questions. Use the word bank to fill in the blanks.

WORD BANK:	sword	loved	acceptable	tree of life	death

1. God refused the clothing of leaves that Adam and Eve made for themselves because God wanted them to know they couldn't do anything to make themselves _____ to God.

2. Is there anything we can do to make ourselves acceptable to God?   YES   NO

3. God killed animals to make clothing for guilty Adam and Eve because God wanted Adam and Eve to be reminded that the punishment for sin is _____.

4. God made clothes for Adam and Eve because, even though they had sinned, God wanted them to know that He _____ them and that He was the only One who could make them acceptable to Him.

5. God put Adam and Eve out of the garden of Eden so they wouldn't be able to eat of the _____ ___ _____ and live forever.

6. God made sure they could not return to the garden of Eden by placing cherubim and a flaming _____ at the entrance to the garden.

7. Can anyone trick or deceive God?   YES   NO

Can you write the word that describes God's perfect nature? This is the word that describes the fact that God never has and never will sin. Everything He does is perfect. He will not accept sin; the penalty for sin is death. God is perfect and sinless.

GOD is _____.

Uncle Don:
Hi, Jessica. Hi, Travis. You kids look pretty happy. What's up?

Jessica:
We've got a surprise for Mom!

Travis:
I'll bet you can't guess what it is, either!

Uncle Don:
You cleaned your rooms.

Jessica:
No, but that was close.

Travis:
Something better than that.

Uncle Don:
I give up. What did you do?

Jessica:
We vacuumed the rug in the living room and cleaned up that stack of things she had in the den. She's really going to be surprised.

Travis:
It wasn't very easy to do with my hand still sore, but I did the vacuuming with the other hand.

Jessica:
And I went through and put all those books on the shelf. I even had to put some stuff back in the closet. I don't know where it all came from.

Travis:
I can hardly wait to see her face. She will really be surprised.

Jessica:
I wonder when she'll be back. Saturday mornings she sometimes takes a while shopping.

Uncle Don:
Kids, I was going to come over and see you in a few minutes. Your mom called before she left and asked me to check in on you. She said she had asked you to clean your rooms.

Travis:
Oh, we know. But they weren't that bad. We got to looking at the floor and then I got the vacuum cleaner.

Jessica:
And I saw that mess in the den so I started there. I like cleaning up other people's messes. It's a lot more fun than cleaning your own room.

Uncle Don:
Kids, I really hate to spoil your fun, but don't you think you should clean your rooms, like your mom asked you?

Jessica:
Well, like Travis said—they aren't that dirty. We couldn't figure out why Mom wanted us to do that first. So we just did something we thought she'd like better. And it **was** more fun.

Uncle Don:
I can tell you've had a good time. I don't think you realized what you were doing, but you've actually disobeyed your mom. And you didn't really believe she meant what she said.

Travis:
But we did something really good!

Jessica:
More important than cleaning our rooms!

Uncle Don:
Jessica, Travis—there's something very serious here. Who gives the instructions in your home?

Travis:
Dad and Mom.

Uncle Don:
Did you listen to your mom and believe her when she told you what she wanted you to do?

Jessica:
No.

Uncle Don:
I feel bad to tell you, but you've not only disobeyed her, but you've done something that you shouldn't have done.

Travis:
All we did was vacuum and put some stuff away!

Uncle Don:
Your mom told me that she has hired the carpet cleaner to come over this afternoon. He's going to do the whole house.

Travis:
You mean I wasted all that effort?

Uncle Don:
And the things you put away she was going to take to the resale shop later today.

Jessica:
Oh, no! I'm sorry!

Uncle Don:
Kids, believing and obeying are extremely important. Let me help you get your rooms cleaned. Then I want you to see something in the Bible. It's the story of Cain and Abel.

God Rejected Cain and His Offering but Accepted Abel and His Offering

Use the WORD BANK to fill in the answers. Circle the right answer to the YES and NO questions.
WORD BANK: belong Deliverer sinner GOD sacrifice believe sinner separated loved

1. Who gives every person his life? _____

2. Because their father Adam sinned, Cain and Abel were born sinners, _____ from God.

3. God accepted Abel's offering because Abel agreed with God that he was a _____. Abel believed that only God could save him from everlasting punishment. He trusted God to send a _____, just as God had promised to Adam and Eve. Abel brought a sheep, killed it, and let its blood run out, just as God had told them to do.

4. A _____ is an offering given to God to agree with God that He is greater than all, He is holy, and to agree that the penalty for sin is death. Does God want us to bring animal sacrifices to Him today?   YES   NO

5. God rejected Cain and his offering because Cain did not agree with God that he was a _____ and that only God could save him from everlasting punishment. Cain did not _____ God. Cain did not bring the offering which God said they must bring.

6. God talked with angry Cain because God _____ Cain and wanted Cain to agree that he was a sinner and that he should bring the correct sacrifice to God.

7. Did Cain believe and agree with God?   YES   NO

8. God will punish all sin against other people because all people rightfully _____to God. When we hurt other people, we are really sinning against God.

When you have finished these questions, look up Proverbs 14:12 and write it on the back of this sheet. Memorize it and then see if you can write it out from memory.

Lesson Scripture: Genesis 4:3-16,25   **LESSON 14** **FIRM FOUNDATIONS** **REVIEW SHEET**

Travis:
Do you remember that kid I told you about who got kicked out of school for stealing?

Uncle Don:
Yes, I remember.

Travis:
Well, he's back in school again.

Uncle Don:
How is his attitude?

Travis:
He's just the same—well, maybe he's worse!

Uncle Don:
What do you mean?

Travis:
He was bragging today about how much stuff he's stolen and not gotten caught.

Jessica:
I've wondered about that.

Uncle Don:
About what, Jessica.

Jessica:
Well, what if a person just doesn't get caught—I mean, if he steals something or does something else bad, but no one knows. I guess he never gets punished, does he.

Uncle Don:
That's not true at all, Jessica. Do you remember what happened to Adam and Eve when they were put out of the garden? Could they have sneaked back in without God seeing them?

Jessica:
No. God sees everything.

Uncle Don:
That's right. He sees and will punish **all** sin.

Travis:
Even the sins nobody knows about?

Jessica:
God knows!

Uncle Don:
Yes, He does. And He has never changed His mind about the penalty for sin. The penalty for sin is death. That's what He told Adam and Eve in the garden, and that's what the penalty is today.

Travis:
How about little sins?

Uncle Don:
Sin is sin, Travis. God is holy. He will not tolerate sin. Sin separates us from God. We are all born sinners. Only God can make a way for sinful man to come to Him.

Jessica:
Uncle Don, I have a question: if sin is so terrible and God is going to punish all sin, why do people keep on sinning?

Uncle Don:
Good question. The Bible tells us that people actually love their sin more than they love God.

Travis:
That's awful!

Uncle Don:
Yes, Travis, it is. The Bible tells us that at one point in history, people became so sinful that all they ever thought about was only evil things.

Jessica:
They must not have had an uncle like you!

Uncle Don:
Well, they did have Noah, and the Bible refers to him as a preacher of righteousness.

Travis:
You mean the "Noah" in the story of the ark?

Uncle Don:
That's the man. God warned the people of Noah's day for 120 years that they must repent. Noah was the man God used to tell them His truth, but the people simply refused to listen. All they cared about was themselves and all their pleasures.

Jessica:
But isn't the story mostly about the ark and the animals?

Uncle Don:
That's only part of the story, Jessica. The important part of the story is God's judgment of sin and his protection of Noah and his family. They believed God and God saved them.

Travis:
I probably shouldn't ask, but is this really a true story? Was there really a flood and an ark?

Uncle Don:
There most certainly was a flood and an ark. It's a very important part of history—when God judged the whole world and saved Noah and his family. You'll be surprised at all the details God gives us in the Bible. Remember, history is **His** Story—God's story! The Bible is true!

Name _____

GOD

judged the world and

delivered Noah

FIND THE HIDDEN MESSAGE!

Use the Word Bank below and write the answers to the questions in the puzzle blanks. Then read the hidden message!

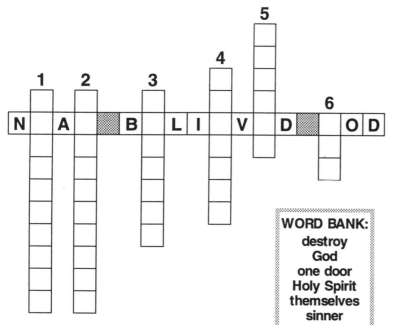

1	2	3	4	5		6	
N	A	B	L	I	V	D	O	D

WORD BANK:
destroy
God
one door
Holy Spirit
themselves
sinner

1. God the _____ _____ reminds people of God's Word and tells people they need to believe in God.

2. Most of the people in Noah's day were interested only in pleasing _____ .

3. God said that if the people would not repent of their sin, He would _____ all of the living things on earth.

4. God told Noah exactly how to build the ark. The ark was to have only _____ _____ .

5. Noah agreed with God that Noah was a _____ . Noah believed that one day God would send a Deliverer to save him from his sins.

6. While Noah was building the ark, he was also warning the people to repent of their sins and to believe _____ .

BONUS BOX!

Once you have found the hidden message, then circle either YES or NO to correctly answer the following questions:

A. Did Noah deserve to be saved from everlasting punishment?   YES   NO

B. Did anyone outside the ark escape death?

YES   NO

FIRM FOUNDATIONS

skit 15

**God Remembered Noah;
God Scattered the Rebels
at the Tower of Babel**
Readers: Uncle Don, Travis, Jessica

Travis:
Uncle Don, I've been thinking about something.

Uncle Don:
What's that, Travis?

Travis:
Well, we've been studying history at school. And then we saw some history programs on TV, and nobody said **anything** about God.

Uncle Don:
Travis, you are an excellent observer. What you say is very true. Men don't believe God, and they don't see any need to include Him and His mighty acts in the story of history.

Jessica:
That silly. God is the greatest of all!

Travis:
Do people really know about Him?

Uncle Don:
Good question. They should. A lot of people have only heard about Him, and they are too busy with their own lives to even think about God.

Jessica:
But He's the most important one of all!

Uncle Don:
He certainly is, Jessica. But down through history, men have refused to listen to God. They don't care about His Word. They even set up false gods for themselves and worship them.

Travis:
But God created everything. He's the greatest.

Uncle Don:
People are more interested in pleasing themselves than they are in knowing the One who created them.

Jessica:
Does God just let them get away with that?

Travis:
Jessica, don't you remember the flood?

Jessica:
Oh! Of course! God judged the whole world then—because they refused to believe Him!

Uncle Don:
God is the main person, the central character of all history. Many scientists are realizing now that the biblical story of the flood explains many things about the earth as we know it today. The whole earth was really changed through the time of the flood.

Travis:
Did the water really cover the whole world?

Uncle Don:
Yes, the Bible tells us that the water covered everything—it rose up to twenty feet above the highest mountains!

Jessica:
That's a **lot** of **water!**

Travis:
What about dinosaurs? How could they have fit into the ark?

Uncle Don:
Have you ever seen a Saint Bernard dog for sale in one of those little cages at the pet shop?

Travis:
How do they ever fit in there?

Jessica:
Oh, Uncle Don! I get it—a puppy—or a baby dinosaur! That would have fit in the ark!

Travis:
That's neat!

Uncle Don:
The wonderful thing about God is that He just continues to be faithful. Even though man became so sinful, God still rescued Noah and his family because they believed God. All through history those who believe in God have been just a small number of people. But God takes care of them and always keeps His promises.

Travis:
What happened after the flood? Did people put their trust in God then?

Uncle Don:
I'm afraid not, Travis. People were sinners, just like now. But God is always righteous and holy and faithful.

Jessica:
Do you think God notices now that people don't think about Him?

Uncle Don:
He knows every thought we think and every word we say. Even though men aren't giving God any mention, God has a record of every man's deeds.

Travis:
That's scary!

Uncle Don:
I want you to see another time when God's judgment of man's sin changed the course of history. Let's look in our Bibles.

 **Scattered the Rebels at the Tower of Babel**

In the empty box write the number of the picture box containing the correct answer!

1. God gave a [ ] as a sign that He would never again destroy the earth.

2. The people after the flood knew about God. They had been told about the flood, and they could see all the things [ ] had created.

3. Most of the people turned away from the truth about God and followed the lies of Satan. Instead of worshipping God, they worshipped idols made to look like [ ] .

4. The people of Babel did not want to be scattered over the world as God had commanded them. They wanted to be the most important. They did not want God to be [ ] in their lives.

5. God saw what they were doing—God knows [ ] .

6. God gave the people different languages so they could not understand each other. Because of this, they began to scatter and move all over the [ ] .

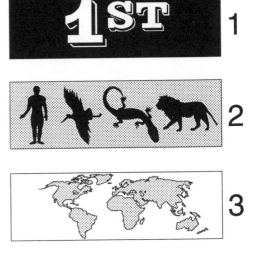

1

2

3

4

everything 5

GOD 6

Jessica:
Where were you last night, Uncle Don? We missed you when we went out for ice cream!

Uncle Don:
Oh, Jessica, I'm sorry! I forgot. I went down to the mall and picked up some books I'd ordered. I sure didn't mean to miss going out with you.

Travis:
That's okay. I ate your ice cream for you!

Jessica:
Uncle Don, I didn't think you'd forget. You are always doing things right.

Uncle Don:
I wish I could say that's true. I sure want to be that way. But I'm not all that faithful. And I really am forgetful. I'm sure glad God isn't like me.

Travis:
What do you mean?

Uncle Don:
God is absolutely **perfect**. He never forgets a promise, and He is always faithful to do everything He says He will do. He can be completely trusted in everything.

Jessica:
Are there lots of promises in the Bible?

Uncle Don:
There are hundreds of them, Jessica.

Jessica:
Hundreds? That's a lot of promises. How can God remember them all?

Uncle Don:
That's no problem for Him. He remembers everything perfectly, and He fulfills every promise at just the right time.

Travis:
Are there any promises in the Bible that haven't yet been fulfilled?

Uncle Don:
Lots of them! But we know that one day they will be fulfilled, exactly as God said they would be.

Jessica:
Has anybody kept track of the ones that have already been fulfilled?

Uncle Don:
Yes, many people have written books about God's promises and their fulfillment; but the best book of all is the Bible itself. Hundreds of promises and their later fulfillment are recorded right in the Bible.

Travis:
Does God ever forget any of the little details?

Uncle Don:
No, God is really amazing. When He fulfills a promise, He keeps every tiny detail. Sometimes it takes a very long time, though, before He is ready to do what He has promised.

Jessica:
I hate to wait.

Travis:
So do I.

Uncle Don:
You're going to have to do a lot of waiting in your lifetime. Are you willing to wait until you are old enough to get married and find a home and have a family of your own? Or would you rather do that right now?

Jessica:
Oh, Uncle Don! You're kidding! Of course I'd wait for that. I'm not ready for that now. I'm too young.

Uncle Don:
You're right. And God knows that, too. And He waits until just the right time to fulfill His promises. Waiting on God and believing Him is part of faith—trusting Him to do what He says He will do—at just the right time.

Travis:
That's hard when you can't see anything happening.

Uncle Don:
It sure is. But that's why faith is so special. The Bible tells us about a man named Abram who was known for his faith.

Jessica:
Why?

Uncle Don:
We'll look at his story in a little while. But the important thing to remember is this: **God is faithful.** People (like me) forget and fail. But God **always** does what He says He will do. Do you remember the first promise about the Deliverer?

Jessica:
You mean the one given in the garden?

Uncle Don:
Yes. God was going to add some wonderful details to that promise as He spoke to Abram. Remember, there was no Bible for Abram to read. God just spoke directly to him!

GOD
Chose, Called, and Guided Abram

Use this WORD BANK to fill in the answers. Circle the right answer to the YES and NO questions.

Deliverer   nation   Abram   no   all   believed   promised

---

1. Because the people rebelled against God and built the tower of Babel, did God give up on His plan to send a Deliverer for all mankind?   YES   NO

2. To ensure that the Deliverer would be born into the world, God chose and called _____ to be the ancestor of the Deliverer.

3. God told Abram to leave his own country and go to the place where God _____ to lead him.

4. When God told Abram and Sarai to go into a different country, they had _____ children.

5. When God told Abram His promises, Abram _____ God. He left his own country and went where God told him to go.

6. *God promised Abram:*

   That his descendants would become a great _____ .

   That God would protect and help Abram.

   That through one of Abram's descendants, _____ people everywhere would be blessed.

   This special descendant would be the _____ .

ABEL, SETH, NOAH, AND ABRAM ALL HAD SOMETHING IN COMMON.
Unscramble the letters and complete the sentence to find the answer!

They all _____ God!

D E I B V E E L

Lesson Scripture: Genesis 11:27-32; 12:1-5; 13:5-13

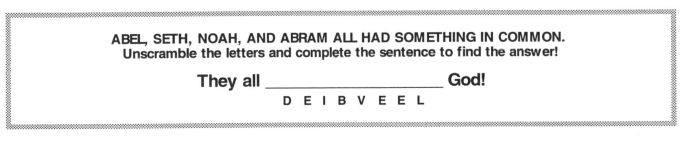

LESSON 17   FIRM FOUNDATIONS   REVIEW SHEET

God Destroyed Sodom and Gomorrah; God Renewed His Promises to Abram

Readers: Uncle Don, Travis, Jessica

Jessica:
Uncle Don, you'll never believe what happened!

Uncle Don:
I can't wait to hear! Tell me!

Travis:
I can't believe it either! You've got to come over and see what Mrs. Hill gave us!

Uncle Don:
I know Mrs. Hill. She used to teach school here years ago. She's been retired now for some time. Her health is failing. So what did she give you?

Jessica:
You just won't believe it! Our teacher announced in the library hour that Mrs. Hill had sent her a note that she had some nice books to give away to a boy or girl who liked to study.

Travis:
You should have heard some of the kids. They said, "Does she have any videos?"

Jessica:
One girl said she had too many books already.

Travis:
Another boy said, "Who's Mrs. Hill anyway. I'll bet she doesn't like the kind of books I like."

Jessica:
But I went to our teacher and asked about Mrs. Hill. Our teacher called Mom, and they talked, and then yesterday Mom said we could visit Mrs. Hill and see what she was talking about.

Travis:
Was I ever surprised!

Jessica:
Me, too! We went up to this big old house and then we were kind of afraid. But Mom had said this was a nice lady, so we knocked at the door.

Travis:
This younger lady came to the door. I guess she is Mrs. Hill's nurse. We went right in to see Mrs. Hill. She is in bed.

Jessica:
But she's so nice! She had the nurse get us something to drink, and then she told us her story.

Travis:
She has some grandchildren, but they never take time to visit her. They used to live around here, and she bought these books for them.

Jessica:
But they and their family didn't want them and didn't even take time to look at them. Uncle Don, she wanted to give them to us!

Uncle Don:
What kind of books were they, Jessica?

Jessica:
A complete set of full-color encyclopedias!

Travis:
With all the extra reference books and an atlas, too! They are beautiful!

Uncle Don:
You are right! I never would have dreamed! That's wonderful!

Jessica:
You know, Uncle Don, I've never felt quite like that. We hadn't done anything for her. We just came to see about the books she'd offered.

Travis:
I didn't even know if we should accept them. I think they must have cost a lot of money.

Uncle Don:
You're right, Travis. They did cost a lot. But she really wanted you to have them, didn't she.

Jessica:
She just amazed us! She kept saying, "I was looking for someone who would just take me at my word."

Travis:
We didn't do anything to deserve those books. Should we really have accepted them?

Uncle Don:
Absolutely. Mrs. Hill bought those books to be used and enjoyed. But her grandchildren refused them. I'm sure it made her very sad. But, like she said—she was looking for someone who would just believe her—believe that she was going to give something good. You took her at her word, and she was glad to give them to you.

Jessica:
I've never had anything so nice.

Travis:
Me neither. And it was all a gift.

Uncle Don:
Kids, we don't deserve the kindness God gives us, either. Most people don't even care about God. He is delighted when someone really believes Him. I want us to look some more at how God showed kindness to Abram. He gave something to Abram that no man could ever deserve. He gave Abram **righteousness**. Even though Abram was a sinner, God accepted him as if Abram were perfectly right.

Name _____

God Destroyed Sodom and Gomorrah

Fill in the blanks using this WORD BANK. Circle the right answer to the "YES and NO" questions.
WORD BANK: believed   all   judge   salt   gracious

1. God will not ignore people's sins. He is the _____ of every person.

2. God waited a long time before He punished the evil people of Sodom and Gomorrah because God is _____. Even today, God gives people opportunity to change their minds about their sin and to put their trust in Him.

3. God is very patient and He is loving and gracious; but He does punish _____ sin.

4. Can anyone stop God from punishing people when He decides that He has given them enough time to change their minds (repent)?   YES   NO

5. Because Lot _____ God and agreed with God that he was a sinner, God rescued Lot and his family.

6. Lot's wife disobeyed God's command and looked back at the burning cities. She was turned into a pillar of _____.

Write Proverbs 15:3 and memorize it. Then try to write it from memory on the back of this sheet.

_____

_____

_____

Lesson Scripture: Genesis 13:14-17;
15:5,6,13-16; 17:1-5,15-17;
18:20,21; 19:1-7,10-17,24-26

LESSON 18 FIRM FOUNDATIONS **REVIEW SHEET**

skit 18

**God Gave Isaac;
God Delivered Isaac from
Death**

Readers: Uncle Don, Travis, Jessica

Travis:
Guess what we found in our new encyclopedia!

Uncle Don:
What did you find, Travis?

Travis:
An article on Abraham! There was even a map of where he came from in Ur and where he moved to in Canaan.

Uncle Don:
I'm glad to hear that he was included in the encyclopedia. Did you know that Abraham lived probably about 4,000 years ago?

Jessica:
I wonder why he's still important enough to be in an encyclopedia.

Travis:
Because he's in the Bible!

Uncle Don:
I wish I could say that's true, Travis. But that really isn't the reason. There are lots of people mentioned in the Bible who are not spoken of in other books. But Abraham is different.

Jessica:
How do you mean?

Travis:
Is it because of what he did?

Uncle Don:
Most of all, it's because of **the promises God gave** to Abraham. And Abraham believed God.

Jessica:
And God accepted him as if he were righteous! But why do people still remember him?

Uncle Don:
The best thing to do is to look in the Bible at some of the promises God gave to Abraham.

Travis:
One promise was that God would make a great nation from Abraham.

Jessica:
And Abraham didn't even have any children then!

Uncle Don:
But look at that last promise in Genesis 12:3.

Travis:
It says that all people on earth would be blessed through Abraham.

Uncle Don:
That includes you and me!

Jessica:
You mean God thought of us way back then?

Uncle Don:
Yes, Jessica, even back then God knew we would be born. God knows everything. And He chose to bring blessing to everyone through the line of Abraham. God's promised Deliverer was going to be one of Abraham's descendants.

Travis:
And God told him that his descendants would be as many as the stars!

Jessica:
How many stars are there, Uncle Don?

Uncle Don:
More than we can count. And scientists are discovering more and more stars as they look through telescopes. God was making a very great and wonderful promise!

Travis:
How did Abraham know for sure that all this was going to happen—especially if he didn't have any children?

Uncle Don:
The Bible tells us that Abraham believed God, even when it seemed impossible. You see, all these things that were promised to Abraham did not depend on Abraham's ability to make them happen. They depended upon **God's ability** to make them happen.

Jessica:
So that's why you said we remember Abraham because of God's promises to him!

Uncle Don:
Exactly. It is not the greatness of Abraham, but the greatness of God that is really shown in Abraham's life. God eventually carried out every one of those promises.

Travis:
But how did He do it if Abraham didn't have any children?

Uncle Don:
Well, God waited until Abraham was one hundred and Sarah was ninety. **Then** God gave them a son!

Jessica:
But that's impossible!

Uncle Don:
But not for God. And with this son, God had still more amazing things to do through Abraham's life. God put Abraham's faith to the test.

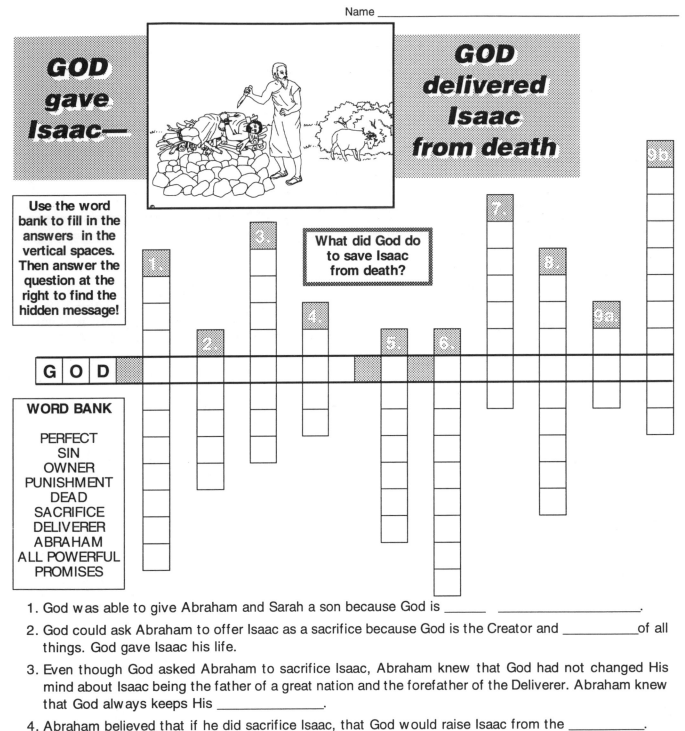

Name _____

GOD gave Isaac—

GOD delivered Isaac from death

Use the word bank to fill in the answers in the vertical spaces. Then answer the question at the right to find the hidden message!

What did God do to save Isaac from death?

G O D

WORD BANK

PERFECT
SIN
OWNER
PUNISHMENT
DEAD
SACRIFICE
DELIVERER
ABRAHAM
ALL POWERFUL
PROMISES

1. God was able to give Abraham and Sarah a son because God is _____ _____.

2. God could ask Abraham to offer Isaac as a sacrifice because God is the Creator and _____ of all things. God gave Isaac his life.

3. Even though God asked Abraham to sacrifice Isaac, Abraham knew that God had not changed His mind about Isaac being the father of a great nation and the forefather of the Deliverer. Abraham knew that God always keeps His _____.

4. Abraham believed that if he did sacrifice Isaac, that God would raise Isaac from the _____.

5. God spoke to _____ and saved Isaac from death. No one else could have saved Isaac.

6. Only God was able to provide a _____ in Isaac's place.

7. The ram was held in the bush by its horns so it would not be harmed. Because God is _____ He will only accept a perfect sacrifice.

8. Abraham called the place where God provided the ram "The Lord will provide." Abraham belived that, just as God provided the ram instead of Isaac, God would also one day provide a _____.

9. The Deliverer would overcome Satan and (9a.) _____ and death and deliver man from Satan's power and everlasting (9b.) _____.

Lesson Scripture: Genesis 21:1-3, 22:1-19

LESSON 19 🔥 FIRM FOUNDATIONS **REVIEW SHEET**

©New Tribes Mission, 1993
Permission given to photocopy for classroom use

Uncle Don:
Hi, Travis. Hi, Jessica. I just opened a bag of cookies. Would you like to have some with me?

Travis:
Sure! We'd love to!

Jessica:
Travis—you just had some cookies at home!

Travis:
I know, but these are different. I like to try different kinds. These are good!

Uncle Don:
So what are you kids doing today?

Jessica:
Oh, we just finished our homework and we decided to come over and visit you.

Travis:
I almost forgot! The main reason we wanted to come over here was to tell you about Dad.

Jessica:
You're right, Travis. I guess we just got to talking and eating cookies. I'd forgotten, too.

Uncle Don:
So what is happening with your dad?

Travis:
He's planning to look for a new job.

Jessica:
One where he doesn't have to travel so much.

Uncle Don:
That's great news!

Travis:
Dad says he misses everybody too much.

Jessica:
He said that he and Mom got married so they could be together, but they hardly see each other.

Travis:
He said he didn't mean to be away so much but it just keeps happening more and more and now he's hardly home at all.

Uncle Don:
Kids, I'm so glad that your dad realizes what is happening. It's so easy to get sidetracked from what we have planned to do.

Jessica:
Dad said it might take a while to find a new job.

Uncle Don:
Yes, it may. But at least he's seeing the need to make a change. You know, I really appreciate your dad. It's not easy to change jobs. And it's not easy to admit that you have gotten away from what you planned.

Travis:
We did that when we came over here! We forgot the main reason why we came!

Uncle Don:
I do that, too. You know something, kids? God **never** gets off track. He never forgets His plans.

Travis:
Not even for a minute?

Uncle Don:
Never. And Satan is continually at work, trying to stop God's plans from succeeding. Do you remember what God promised in the garden when Adam and Eve first sinned?

Jessica:
God promised to send a Deliverer.

Travis:
Someone who would defeat Satan!

Uncle Don:
Yes, a Deliverer who would rescue people from sin and Satan and death. That's the greatest need man has. Sin separates man from God.

Jessica:
Can Satan stop God from carrying out His plans?

Uncle Don:
No, Jessica, he can't. Satan has tried—remember how Abel died? But God gave Seth in his place. God is greater than all. God has had one great, master plan to save people from Satan and sin and death. He passed on His promises from one generation to another, from father to son.

Travis:
Did these men know God's plan?

Uncle Don:
Some of them sure did, at least in part. God gave His promise of a Deliverer to Abraham, then later he gave the same promise to Isaac, and later on to Isaac's son, Jacob.

Jessica:
So Abraham knew that Isaac **had to** stay alive—it was part of God's promise—Abraham had to have descendants to keep the line of the Deliverer! Now I understand.

Uncle Don:
God keeps every promise; He finishes every plan. The Bible is an amazing story, because God is completely faithful!

Name _____

GOD Rejected Esau and Chose Jacob

Use this
WORD BANK
to fill in the
answers to the
questions.

**BIBLE
GOD
CHANGES
DELIVERER
ALWAYS
ISRAEL
HEAVEN**

1. Draw a line from each name below to the words that correctly describe that person.

   JACOB

   ESAU

   - lived for the present and for the things he wanted for himself

   - did not care about God's promises

   - admitted that he was a sinner and trusted in God

   - refused to admit that he was a sinner and did not trust in God

   - valued God's promises about the Deliverer

2. To Adam and Eve and to Abraham, God gave promises about the Deliverer. God never _____. He _____ keeps His promises.

3. In his dream, Jacob saw a stairway (or ladder) resting on the earth with its top reaching to _____. God's angels were walking up and down the ladder, and _____ stood above the ladder.

4. God gave this dream to Jacob to show him that the Deliverer, who would be a descendant of Jacob, would be like the stairway connecting earth to Heaven. Through this _____, people could be brought into oneness with God.

5. God gave a new name to Jacob. He called him _____.

6. God spoke to Jacob in a dream. Today, God speaks to us through the _____.

Lesson Scripture: Genesis 25:19-21,24-27;
28:10-15; 29:1;
37:1-14,18-20,24,28; 39:1

LESSON 20 Firm FOUNDATIONS **REVIEW SHEET**

Jessica:
Oh, Uncle Don! I just can't believe what's happened. Remember what we told you about Dad wanting to look for another job—so he wouldn't have to be away from home so much?

Uncle Don:
Yes, I remember. What happened?

Travis:
Now he's going to have to be gone for two months, and he has to do it, or he could lose his job.

Jessica:
And he can't take time now to look for another job. He has to leave tomorrow.

Uncle Don:
Kids, I'm so sorry. How is your mom doing?

Travis:
She's really upset. She said she can't understand how God could let it happen.

Uncle Don:
I need to talk with your mom and try to encourage her. You know, it may be the very best thing that could happen.

Travis:
What?

Jessica:
How could it be good? Dad will just be gone more, and he won't have a chance to look for another job.

Uncle Don:
Do you remember that word we learned a while back—the word that describes the fact that God is greater than all?

Travis:
You mean "sovereign"?

Uncle Don:
Good, Travis. Yes, that's the word. It means that God is the highest authority. He is the one who has the final say on things, and He knows exactly how to work everything out according to His plan—even when things look terrible.

Jessica:
But I don't understand. Doesn't God want us to see Dad? Doesn't God want Dad to be home?

Uncle Don:
Of course He does, Jessica. But sometimes we have to wait a while before even good things

happen. Sometimes God has other things He wants us and others to learn along the way.

Travis:
I don't like waiting.

Jessica:
I miss Dad already, and he's not even gone.

Uncle Don:
Kids, I want you to think about something. How did the future look when Adam and Eve sinned?

Travis:
Not good. The penalty for sin is death.

Uncle Don:
But what did God do?

Jessica:
He promised a Deliverer.

Uncle Don:
Did He send the Deliverer right away?

Travis:
No.

Uncle Don:
How did things look when God sent the flood?

Jessica:
Awful! But God saved Noah and everyone in the ark.

Uncle Don:
What about Abraham? He didn't have any children until he was one hundred.

Travis:
And then there was Isaac. I still can't believe what happened to him and how God saved him!

Uncle Don:
God is the **only one** who can save us! Do you think this is the end of your hopes for your dad to get a job that will keep him closer to home?

Travis:
Well, it seemed like it. But I guess it really isn't.

Jessica:
I'd still like him to stay home right now.

Uncle Don:
So would I. But I think you'll really appreciate the story we are about to study. God did another very amazing thing, all part of His plan to make a way for people to be saved from their sins. This time, God allowed an innocent man to stay in jail for two years!

Travis:
You're kidding!

Uncle Don:
No, it really happened, and God used it for good.

God promoted Joseph and took Israel into Egypt

WORD BANK
Use these words to fill in the blanks in the questions below. Circle the right answer to the YES and NO question.
LEADERSHIP
GOD
BELIEVED
FOOD
ISRAELITES
GOD
BELIEVED
GOD

1. _____ took care of Joseph in prison.

2. Joseph was a sinner, but he _____ God.

3. _____ gave Joseph the ability to understand Pharaoh's dreams.

4. Is it possible for God to do great things in a country where people do not believe in Him?

   YES   NO

5. God gave Joseph wisdom to interpret Pharaoh's dreams so that Pharaoh would give Joseph a position of _____, just as God had shown Joseph in his dreams.

6. Jacob took all of his family down to live in Egypt because he heard that his son Joseph was there; there was plenty of _____ there, and Pharaoh invited him to come. But, most important, _____ planned for all this to happen.

7. The descendants of Abraham, Isaac, and Jacob were called _____.

8. Joseph was able to live the way he did because he _____ God.

Write out Proverbs 21:1 and then memorize it. See if you can write it from memory on the back of this sheet. _____

_____

_____

_____

Jessica:
Guess what, Uncle Don? I found the name "Israel" on the front page of the newspaper!

Travis:
And I found Israel in the encyclopedia!

Uncle Don:
I'm glad to hear that you kids are keeping your eyes open and learning! Do you remember the very first things we learned about Israel when we started our Bible study?

Travis:
No.

Jessica:
Was it about the people that God used to write down the Bible?

Uncle Don:
Right, Jessica! God chose Jewish men, that is, Israelites, to write down His Word. All but one of the men were Jews.

Travis:
Oh, I remember now. You said that Israel was like God's microphone to announce His Word to the world.

Uncle Don:
That's right, Travis. And Israel is still very important and very much in the news today.

Jessica:
What's it like there today?

Uncle Don:
Well, if you went to visit Israel, you could still see many of the places named and talked about in the Bible.

Travis:
I'd really like to visit there!

Jessica:
Me, too!

Uncle Don:
Some of Israel is very modern. But some of it is still very much like it was in Bible times. A lot of people live in Israel, and many of them are Jewish—people who trace their family history back to Bible times. Remember, the Israelites or Jews trace their history back to Abraham, and to Jacob, whom God called Israel.

Jessica:
How long ago did Abraham and Jacob live?

Travis:
I know that answer! Abraham lived almost 4,000 years ago. And Jacob was his grandson.

Jessica:
That's a long time ago.

Uncle Don:
We're going to study about what happened to the Israelite people after they went down into Egypt.

Travis:
We still hear about Egypt today, too!

Uncle Don:
Yes, and some of the things mentioned in the Bible can still be seen there, too.

Travis:
I never knew that all this stuff in the Bible was real. I think I like learning about all these places and people.

Uncle Don:
It really is interesting, Travis. But the amazing and wonderful thing about the Bible is that it tells us about what God is like—who He is.

Jessica:
I never knew that He had such big plans—and I never knew how long He waited to make them happen.

Travis:
I think it's neat! Everything He promised, He made it happen—even though it took a long time sometimes.

Uncle Don:
The Israelites moved down to Egypt during a famine, when Joseph was the ruler there—that was all part of God's plan.

Jessica:
I liked Joseph's story!

Uncle Don:
Me, too. But after many years, Joseph got old and died, and another Pharaoh ruled Egypt. He was very unkind to the Israelites.

Travis:
Did God let him get away with it?

Uncle Don:
For a while. But then the Israelites began to cry out to God for help. God wanted them to admit that they couldn't help themselves. Only He could help them.

Travis:
I'm seeing something else in the Bible—it's not only real, like a history book; it's, well—like real people today. We need God, too, don't we!

Name _____

GOD Preserved Israel Enslaved in Egypt; GOD Called Moses

1. The king of Egypt was _____ of the Israelites because there were so many of them. He decided to make the Israelites his _____.

2. _____ was guiding the evil king in his plans. Satan knew that God had promised Abraham, Isaac, and Jacob that one of their descendants would be the _____.

3. God allowed Pharaoh's daughter to adopt _____ because God was going to work through him to deliver the Israelites from slavery.

4. Could the Israelites or Moses himself free the Israelites from slavery?   YES   NO

5. Who is the only one who can deliver a person from Satan's control? _____

6. God delivered the Israelites because He is _____; and because He had promised to _____ that he would make of him a great nation and that through him the Deliverer would come into the world.

7. When Moses saw the burning bush, the bush was not burned up because _____ was in the bush.

BONUS QUESTION: What is God's special name that means that He is the one who needs nothing; the one who has existed from before the beginning? (This is the name that God told Moses to tell the people when they asked who had sent him. You will find it in Exodus 3:14.)

_____ _____

God Sent Plagues on Egypt; God Passed Over Israel

Readers: Uncle Don, Travis, Jessica

Travis:
Uncle Don, did you hear about the tornado watch?

Uncle Don:
Yes, I heard it on the car radio on the way home from work. I was just about to call your mom and tell her.

Jessica:
Will we have a tornado?

Uncle Don:
I don't know. But when we have a watch issued like that it means that there's real danger of a tornado forming in the area. It's important to keep up with the news in case a tornado is sighted.

Travis:
I heard one of the guys at school today saying that he would never listen to any of those warnings. He said nothing ever happens, anyway.

Uncle Don:
That's a very dangerous attitude, Travis. People die because of refusing to listen to warnings.

Jessica:
How do you mean?

Uncle Don:
Well, just an example: several years ago scientists began to give warnings that a mountain was about to have a volcanic eruption.

Travis:
A volcano!

Uncle Don:
Yes, but this mountain had not erupted for a long time—probably hundreds of years. People were living up on its slopes and some people were up there hiking and just enjoying themselves.

Jessica:
So did most of the people leave?

Uncle Don:
Very few of them wanted to leave. They were just like the boy you mentioned. They thought nothing would happen, in spite of the fact that the warnings were coming very frequently. Some of them did leave, though.

Travis:
You mean some of them decided to stay?

Uncle Don:
Yes, they did. They just didn't believe that anything would happen. But it did.

Travis:
You mean the volcano erupted?

Uncle Don:
Yes. It was even more terrible than they could have imagined. Several people were killed—people who could have been saved if they had listened to the warnings and followed the instructions to leave immediately.

Jessica:
That's terrible. They didn't have to die, did they!

Uncle Don:
No. They had been warned, over and over—just like the people in Noah's time.

Travis:
I wonder why people act like that?

Uncle Don:
It's part of being sinful. We are all a little that way—not wanting to be told what to do. It's a form of rebellion.

Jessica:
Like Satan rebelled?

Uncle Don:
Yes. One of the best examples of rebellion is the Pharaoh who ruled in Egypt during the time of Moses. This Pharaoh just refused to listen to God.

Travis:
Did he know who God was?

Uncle Don:
Pharaoh worshipped false gods. He didn't want to know about the one true God.

Jessica:
Why didn't he want to know God?

Uncle Don:
Some people are very proud of themselves. They refuse to listen to anyone. They don't realize that they are totally dependent upon God for everything. They refuse to believe that He is the Creator.

Travis:
Does God let a person get away with that?

Uncle Don:
No, but sometimes He lets a person go on like that for quite a while. God gives opportunity for sinners to repent. But He judges all sin. None of God's warnings are empty. He does what He says in His Word.

Jessica:
So did Pharaoh finally listen to God?

Uncle Don:
No, he didn't. God judged Pharaoh's rebellion, and He did it in a way that we still remember today. Let's read this story in the Bible.

GOD
sent plagues on Egypt

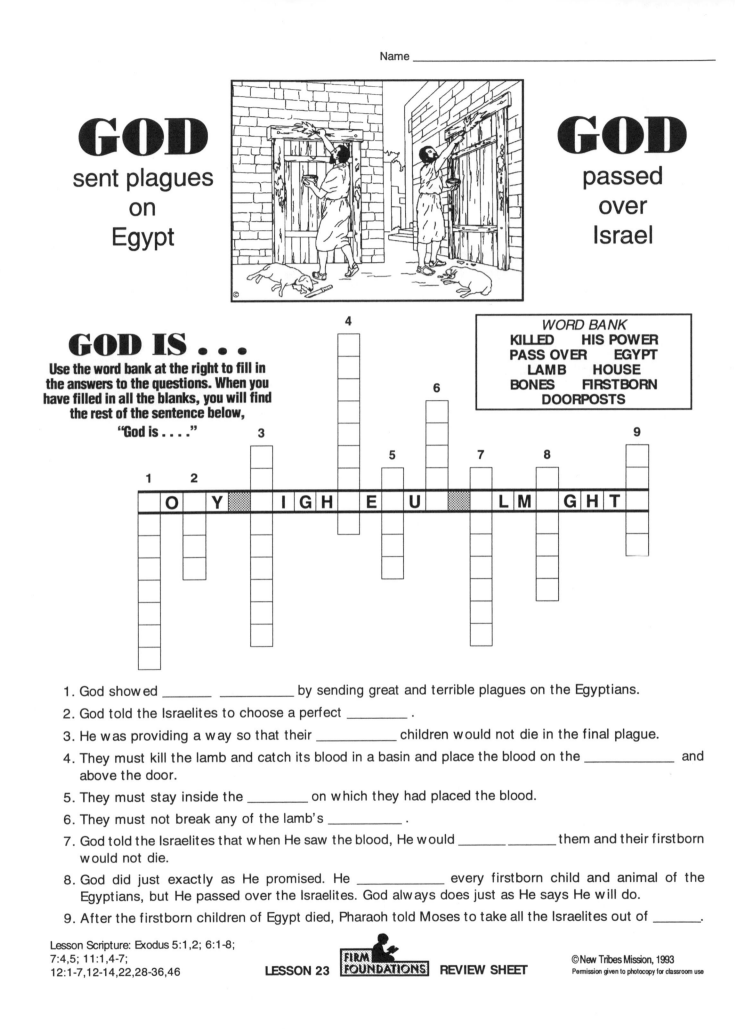

GOD
passed over Israel

GOD IS . . .

Use the word bank at the right to fill in the answers to the questions. When you have filled in all the blanks, you will find the rest of the sentence below,

"God is . . . ."

WORD BANK
KILLED   HIS POWER
PASS OVER   EGYPT
LAMB   HOUSE
BONES   FIRSTBORN
DOORPOSTS

Crossword grid with across answer: O _ Y _ _ I G H _ E U _ _ L M _ G H T (numbered 1-9)

1. God showed _____ _____ by sending great and terrible plagues on the Egyptians.

2. God told the Israelites to choose a perfect _____ .

3. He was providing a way so that their _____ children would not die in the final plague.

4. They must kill the lamb and catch its blood in a basin and place the blood on the _____ and above the door.

5. They must stay inside the _____ on which they had placed the blood.

6. They must not break any of the lamb's _____ .

7. God told the Israelites that when He saw the blood, He would _____ _____ them and their firstborn would not die.

8. God did just exactly as He promised. He _____ every firstborn child and animal of the Egyptians, but He passed over the Israelites. God always does just as He says He will do.

9. After the firstborn children of Egypt died, Pharaoh told Moses to take all the Israelites out of _____ .

Lesson Scripture: Exodus 5:1,2; 6:1-8; 7:4,5; 11:1,4-7; 12:1-7,12-14,22,28-36,46

FIRM FOUNDATIONS

LESSON 23   **REVIEW SHEET**

Jessica:
Uncle Don! Guess what! Dad has a new job!

Travis:
Right here in town! And he won't have to travel all the time!

Uncle Don:
That's wonderful! I thought your dad was out of town for a couple of months. Did he come back?

Jessica:
No! That's what's so great! He met a man at one of his meetings, and this man wants Dad to set up a business for him, right here, and he wants Dad to manage it!

Travis:
And he never would have met that man if he hadn't gone on that trip!

Jessica:
You should hear Mom! She is really excited.

Uncle Don:
I remember how upset she was when your dad had to take that long trip—right after he'd decided to look for a job that would let him be at home more.

Jessica:
I know. We all thought it wasn't fair. Mom was upset with God for letting it happen.

Travis:
But you should have seen her when Dad told her over the phone! She was so happy!

Jessica:
Dad never could have known about that man if he hadn't gone out there. Do you think God knew?

Uncle Don:
Of course He did, Jessica. God knows everything.

Travis:
I wish **we'd** known!

Jessica:
Mom said she was sorry for being mad at God about Dad having to go on that trip.

Uncle Don:
This was a hard time for your whole family, but it's really obvious that God was the One who provided the job. God wants us to trust Him for everything. Do you remember what God did for the Israelites when they were in slavery?

Travis:
He sent the plagues on Egypt!

Uncle Don:
God was showing them and us just how great He is. He wanted them to trust only in Him. Only He could make a way for them to escape.

Jessica:
They'd been slaves for a long time. They really deserved some help!

Uncle Don:
They certainly **needed** help, and God helped them because He loved them and because of His promises. But they were no more deserving of God's help than we are.

Jessica:
What do you mean?

Uncle Don:
They were sinners, Jessica, just like us. They deserved death. That was why God had them kill the lambs and put the blood on the doorposts—when God saw the blood, He passed over them.

Travis:
And not one of their firstborn died!

Uncle Don:
God was gracious to them. They could never have escaped Egypt without God's help. God wanted them to trust Him for everything—just like He wants us to trust Him for everything!

Jessica:
How did they get out of Egypt?

Travis:
Couldn't they just walk away after all of that?

Uncle Don:
No, there were still enemies to face, and desert country with no food or water. Only God could make a way for them. Besides, there were probably around two and a half million Israelites!

Travis:
That's as many as in a big city! How did God do it?

Uncle Don:
First, God opened up a way right through the sea, and all of the Israelites walked out on dry ground.

Travis:
I'd like to have seen that!

Jessica:
But what did they do in the desert? How did they get food and water?

Uncle Don:
There was nothing they could do to help themselves. They had to trust completely in God for everything. Let's read about it.

Name _____

GOD Delivered Israel at the Red Sea

GOD Provided Food and Water In The Desert

Fill in the blanks using this WORD BANK. Circle the right answer to the "YES and NO" questions.

God	save themselves	complained	gracious	cloud	created	all-powerful
	Canaan	pillar of fire	God	Deliverer		

1. The Lord guided the Israelites by a _____ during the day and a _____

   _____ _____ at night.

2. God was guiding the Israelites back to the land of _____, the land He had promised

   to Abraham, Isaac, and Jacob.

3. God protected Israel because God is _____. God always keeps His promises.

   He had promised to send a _____ for the whole world through Israel.

4. When the Israelites saw Pharaoh's armies coming after them, they blamed Moses. They could

   not _____ _____ from the Egyptians. They should have called on

   _____.

5. God was able to open up the Red Sea for them because He _____ it and because

   He is _____.

6. Can anyone make a way to deliver himself from God's punishment for sin?   YES   NO

7. When the Israelites ran out of food and water, they _____ instead of asking

   _____ to help them.

8. Did Israel deserve for God to give them food and water?   YES   NO

CAN YOU FIND THE FOOD GOD GAVE THE ISRAELITES?
Unscramble these letters to find the answer. Check your answer in Exodus 16:35.
A M N A N _____

Lesson Scripture: Exodus 13:17,18,21;
14:5-7,10-16,19-31; 16:1-3,11-15,35;
17:1-6   LESSON 24 FIRM FOUNDATIONS REVIEW SHEET   © New Tribes Mission, 1993
Permission given to photocopy for classroom use

Travis:
What are you doing, Jessica?

Jessica:
I'm memorizing. Don't interrupt me.

Travis:
What are you memorizing?

Jessica:
Travis, don't interrupt me! I'm memorizing the Ten Commandments.

Travis:
Well, you don't need to be so touchy about it!

Jessica:
I'm not touchy! I'm just writing these so I'll remember them—and you're interrupting me.

Travis:
You're writing on that new stationery Mom told us not to use. I'm going to tell Mom!

Jessica:
Oh, Travis! Stop it! Don't tell her that—just tell her I just got some like hers at the store.

Travis:
Jessica, that's a lie!

Jessica:
Not really. I'll get some more sometime maybe. Now stop bothering me!

Uncle Don:
Hi, kids.

Travis:
Hi, Uncle Don.

Jessica:
Oh, I didn't see you come over here. Hi.

Uncle Don:
What are you writing, Jessica?

Jessica:
Something really good! I'm writing down the Ten Commandments so I can memorize them. I don't ever want to break any of God's commandments!

Uncle Don:
Really? I hate to tell you this, but no one but God Himself is able to fully carry out His commandments.

Jessica:
What do you mean? I always keep the Ten Commandments, I think.

Travis:
Me, too. Wait a minute. What did you say, Uncle Don?

Uncle Don:
I said that no one but God is able to perfectly keep His commandments. God gave His commandments so we people could see just how sinful we really are.

Jessica:
But that's why I'm memorizing them. I want to know them so I'll never break them.

Uncle Don:
That's just about how the Israelites felt about God's commandments—they were sure they could keep them and not break them.

Travis:
Were they able to do that?

Uncle Don:
No, the Law demands perfect obedience. No one obeys God perfectly all the time. We are all born sinners, and we sin.

Jessica:
But Uncle Don, I've never killed anybody!

Travis:
Me, neither.

Uncle Don:
Have you ever disobeyed your parents?

Travis:
That's not fair! Of course I have.

Jessica:
I obey!

Travis:
Jessica! You do not! You just took Mom's stationery she told us not to use, and you're always whining about what Mom tells you to do.

Jessica:
But that's just little stuff.

Uncle Don:
God's Law demands **perfect** obedience. How about lying—have you ever told a lie?

Jessica:
Of course not!

Travis:
Jessica, that's a lie! You just told me to tell a lie to Mom!

Jessica:
That was just a little lie.

Uncle Don:
Jessica, God's Word says that by doing just one small sin you are guilty of having broken **all** of God's commandments.

Name _____

GOD SPOKE FROM MOUNT SINAI

Circle the right answers to the yes and no questions.
Use the word bank to fill in the answers to the rest of the questions.

WORD BANK: sinners proud sin Moses sinners Bible separation holy

1. God planned to give Israel His commandments to prove to them that they were _____ and that they were not able to please God nor to be accepted by Him through their own efforts.

2. Israel had forgotten that many times they had doubted God and sinned against Him. They were _____ and self-confident.

3. God told Moses to put a boundary around the mountain to remind the people that God is _____. Sinners cannot come near to Him because God hates sin.

4. The mountain shook, and there was thunder and lightning. God wanted the people to know that He is almighty and He punishes _____.

5. God chose _____ to be his messenger to the Israelites.

6. Today, we hear God's message from the _____.

7. The punishment for breaking even one of God's commandments is everlasting _____ from God and punishment in the Lake of Fire.

8. It is impossible for any person to perfectly obey God's commandments because we are all born _____, separated from God and unable to please Him.

9. Did God think that the Israelites would be able to obey His commandments? YES NO

10. Did the Israelites think they could obey God's commandments? YES NO

11. Will God accept us if we do our best and try to obey His commandments? YES NO

Lesson Scripture:
Exodus 19:1-13,16-20; 20:1,2

LESSON 25 FIRM FOUNDATIONS REVIEW SHEET

© New Tribes Mission, 1993
Permission given to photocopy for classroom use

Jessica:
Uncle Don, Travis and I still don't understand what good the Law is if nobody can keep it.

Uncle Don:
God tells us in Romans that the Law is like a teacher, showing us how sinful we really are.

Jessica:
I guess that's what happened to me the day I was lying and disobeying Mom. I thought those were just little things. I didn't think they were really sins.

Uncle Don:
I remember. You even thought you were obeying the Ten Commandments, didn't you?

Jessica:
I did until you showed me what the commandments really meant. Then I knew I had broken them.

Uncle Don:
Hi, Travis! Where have you been?

Travis:
In the basement.

Jessica:
You are a mess!

Travis:
What do you mean, I'm a mess?

Jessica:
Your face—it's all dirty!

Travis:
No, it's not! I just washed.

Jessica:
You really look funny, Travis. You're all greasy.

Travis:
But I just washed.

Uncle Don:
Travis, you'd better take a look in the mirror. There's one right there in the garage by the sink.

Travis:
I can't believe it! I thought I got all cleaned up! We were looking through some old stuff. I went and washed, but I didn't look in the mirror.

Jessica:
You didn't believe me, did you!

Travis:
No. But I had to believe the mirror!

Uncle Don:
That's a good example of how we see ourselves most of the time. We think we are just fine until we really see ourselves clearly reflected in God's Law.

Jessica:
Kind of like I was that day. I really didn't think I had broken God's Law.

Travis:
I still don't get it—why did God give the Ten Commandments if we couldn't keep them?

Uncle Don:
Travis, it's just like the mirror you just looked into—you thought you were clean until you saw what you actually looked like. We are just like that—from our side, we think we aren't sinners.

Jessica:
But the Ten Commandments show us we really are sinners.

Travis:
Couldn't God just **tell us** we are sinners?

Uncle Don:
He has, Travis. But people don't want to listen. They don't read God's Word. And even when they do, they sometimes fail to see that it applies to them.

Travis:
But is the Law really good if it only shows people how bad they are?

Uncle Don:
We **need to know** that we are sinners. Our sins separate us from God. He wants us to see that we are completely unable to help ourselves. God wants us to admit that we are sinners and trust only in Him to make a way to save us.

Jessica:
Wouldn't it be easier if we could just **do** something to be good? It's not easy to trust.

Uncle Don:
God wants us to come to Him by faith.

Travis:
I wish I understood. What else does the Law do?

Uncle Don:
The Law reminds us that God is holy—**He's perfect!** He will not allow sinful man in His presence.

Travis:
Why did God do it that way?

Uncle Don:
God's ways are absolutely perfect. It is up to Him to decide everything. He loves us, and He alone knows what is best. The Law is perfect because God is perfect. He is sovereign—He has the final say on everything!

Name _____

GOD GAVE THE 10 COMMANDMENTS

Circle the right answers to the YES and NO questions. Use the WORD BANK to fill in the blanks.
WORD BANK: coveting   hates   lying   sinning   bodies   created   punished

1. Does God care if people worship or serve anyone or anything besides Him?   YES   NO

2. Is it all right to make an image of something or worship anything else we have made or which God has created?   YES   NO

3. Does God care what we think about Him and what we say about Him?   YES   NO

4. God commanded that the Israelites rest on the seventh day of the week so they would remember that He _____ everything in six days and on the seventh day He rested.

5. When we do not obey our parents, we are _____ against God.

6. God says that a person who _____ another person is like a murderer.

7. God says that a man and wife are to have a special relationship with each other. Their

    _____ belong to God and to each other, but not to anyone else.

8. God allows people to own things. Stealing is sin, and all sin will be _____.

9. God always speaks and thinks the truth. All _____ is sin.

10. If we envy another person and want what they have, we are guilty of _____.

    That was Satan's sin. He was envious of God and wanted His position.

11. Can anyone obey the Ten Commandments?   YES   NO

BONUS QUESTION:

What if a person wanted to do the wrong thing, but never did it because he was afraid he would be caught—would God see that as sin, even though the person never **did** the wrong thing he wanted to do?   YES   NO
On the back of this paper write WHY you believe this would or would not be sin. _____

Lesson Scripture: Exodus 20:3-17   **LESSON 26**  FIRM FOUNDATIONS **REVIEW SHEET**

The Tabernacle

Readers: Uncle Don, Travis, Jessica

Uncle Don:
Hi, kids. Travis, you look like you're deep in thought.

Travis:
Oh, hi, Uncle Don. I was just thinking about what you told us about God and how He won't accept anything we do to take care of our sins. Everyone is really in trouble!

Uncle Don:
You're right, Travis.

Travis:
How does anybody ever come to God? I mean, if God is holy, and He is perfect, we couldn't ever get near Him. He wouldn't want us.

Uncle Don:
He certainly does want us—He wants us very much! Do you remember how the Israelites thought they could obey God's commandments?

Jessica:
Travis and I thought we could, too. But we can't.

Uncle Don:
Neither could the Israelites. But God still wanted them to come to Him, so He made a way for them.

Travis:
While they were still out in the desert?

Uncle Don:
Yes, God wanted to be with them, every step of the way. And He wanted them to know how to come to Him by faith.

Jessica:
He was right there in the cloud!

Travis:
And a pillar of fire at night!

Uncle Don:
But God wanted them to learn even more about Him. Once He had given them His commandments, He knew they would need His mercy.

Travis:
What's mercy?

Uncle Don:
Mercy is God providing a way for sinners to escape the punishment they deserve for breaking His laws.

Jessica:
Did the Israelites break God's laws right away?

Uncle Don:
Yes, Jessica, they certainly did. God had warned them of the seriousness of breaking His commandments, but they thought they were able to keep them.

Travis:
So what did God do to make a way for them to escape their punishment?

Uncle Don:
God instructed Moses to build a tabernacle.

Jessica:
A what?

Uncle Don:
A tabernacle. Tabernacle just means a dwelling place—a place to live. God wanted a special place to live among the Israelites so that He could show them the mercy they needed.

Travis:
You mean He wanted to do that even though they were sinning?

Uncle Don:
Yes, Travis, He did. He gave Moses exact instructions on how to build the tabernacle. Every detail had to be done God's way.

Jessica:
Just like when God told Noah how to build the ark!

Uncle Don:
Exactly! Only God can make a way for us to come to Him, and that's what He was doing for the Israelites. The tabernacle would be the place where God would meet with them and show mercy.

Travis:
How did God meet with all of those people?

Uncle Don:
God appointed special representatives from among the people. He called these men priests.

Jessica:
Could anybody be a priest?

Uncle Don:
No, God made the choice. The priests were sinners, too, so God had to make a way for them to come to Him. Everything had to be done God's way.

Travis:
Do we know what the tabernacle looked like?

Uncle Don:
God tells us quite a bit about it. Every detail was important. This was not only a building plan, but also God's plan of mercy for the Israelites. He gave these instructions to Moses about 3,500 years ago! Let's read them in our Bibles.

In this picture of the inside of the tabernacle, each part is numbered and named. Use the names listed to fill in the blanks in the sentences below.

1. **holy place**

2. **most holy place (holy of holies)**

3. **ark of the covenant**

4. **mercy seat (atonement cover)**

5. **curtain (veil)**

6. **priest**

The Tabernacle

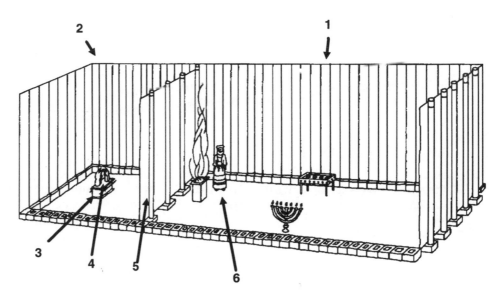

The tabernacle was God's special house where He could live among the Israelites and show them mercy. God told Moses that the people must build the tabernacle exactly according to God's instructions. The larger, first room inside the tabernacle was called the _____ _____ or the separate place. The second room was called the _____ _____ _____ or the holy of holies. Inside this room, God told Moses to place the _____ ____ _____ _____. On top of the ark was the _____ _____. Here God promised to live with the Israelites and show them mercy. The high _____ was the only one allowed to enter the most holy place, and he could only enter once a year. He had to sacrifice a perfect animal, go inside the thick _____ that separated the two rooms, and sprinkle some of the animal's blood on the mercy seat. If the priest did this, God would forgive the Israelites' sins and hold off punishment of their sins for another year. Everything had to be done exactly as God said to do it. The blood of animals [circle one] would / would not pay for sins. The only payment for sin is the death of the sinner.

Lesson Scripture: Exodus 24:12-18; 25:1-11,17-22; 26:31-33; 27:1,2; 28:1; 39:42,43; 40:17,34,35; Leviticus 1:1-5; 16:2,3

LESSON 27 FIRM FOUNDATIONS **REVIEW SHEET**

Travis:
What are you doing with that paint, Uncle Don?

Jessica:
He's stirring it. Can't you see?

Uncle Don:
Actually, I'm mixing a new color. I have some tinting colors and I'm trying to match the shade of blue on this little paper.

Travis:
Let me help! It doesn't look blue enough.

Uncle Don:
Well, if you want to stir for a while, that would be a big help. But trust me, that's enough blue. It just needs to be stirred. Let's see—I need to look over there in the drawers to see if I can find my smaller brushes.

Jessica:
Can I help you look?

Uncle Don:
Sure, Jessica. Thanks, kids. I really appreciate your wanting to help. I don't have a lot of time to finish this little project this afternoon.

Jessica:
Are these the brushes?

Uncle Don:
Those are the ones! Thanks, Jessica. Now, let's see how Travis is . . . Oh, no! You didn't!

Travis:
I was just trying to help.

Uncle Don:
Why did you add more blue? All I asked you to do was stir.

Travis:
It didn't look blue enough to me.

Uncle Don:
You didn't believe what I told you, did you?

Travis:
I'm sorry. I just didn't think it was right.

Jessica:
Can you just add some more white?

Uncle Don:
I'm afraid not, Jessica. That gallon of paint will just have to be thrown out.

Travis:
I'm sorry. I really thought I was right.

Uncle Don:
I forgive you, Travis. Fortunately, it's just a can of paint. But maybe we can learn something from it.

Jessica:
How do you mean, Uncle Don?

Uncle Don:
Well, what Travis did is a lot like the way we people do a lot of things: we refuse to believe clear instructions. Then we do what we think is right, only to find out we've really done something very wrong.

Travis:
I said I was sorry.

Uncle Don:
And I forgave you. But think about it. What if I had told you something with more serious consequences. Do you remember the time you were cut on your dad's saw? Being sorry didn't change the fact that you had a serious injury.

Travis:
I see what you mean. I still have some trouble with that thumb.

Uncle Don:
And it could have been something even more serious than that.

Jessica:
Like what?

Uncle Don:
I'm thinking about the things God tells us to believe. And I'm thinking about the Israelites. God had men write down the exact things that happened to the Israelites so we could be warned.

Jessica:
Warned about what?

Uncle Don:
God wants us to know that the penalty for sin is death. He also wants us to know that the only way for us to come to Him is by faith, believing God.

Travis:
God did a lot for the Israelites. Did they ever believe Him?

Uncle Don:
Very, very few of them did, even though God did miracle after miracle for them. But there were always a few who believed—even in the desert.

Jessica:
That must have been really hard out there.

Uncle Don:
It really was, Jessica. They couldn't depend on how they felt or what they saw. God just wanted them to depend totally upon Him for everything.

Israel did not believe God, so He judged them

But some believed Him, and He delivered them

Fill in the answers to the questions using the words in this WORD BANK.

look at	God	believed	sin	believe	merciful	died
		promises	die	promises		

1. Ten of the spies thought that Israel should not try to enter Canaan because they saw the giants in the land and they did not _____ God's promises.

2. But Joshua and Caleb believed God and trusted in His _____ to give them the land.

3. God said that all who did not believe His promises would _____ in the wilderness. They would not enter Canaan. But Joshua and Caleb, who believed God, and also the children of the Israelites would be able to enter the land. God always keeps His _____.

4. When the Israelites complained, God sent poisonous snakes among them. The Israelites were bitten by the snakes and _____. Satan is like a serpent who has bitten everyone with _____, so that all people die.

5. God told Moses to make a brazen (brass) serpent and put it on a pole. If anyone who was bitten by a snake would just _____ _____ the serpent on the pole, he would be healed.

9. It was _____ who healed the people who looked at the serpent. He healed them because He is loving and _____ and because they _____ Him.

Unscramble the letters and find the hidden message!

_____ GOD!

E V I E B L E

Lesson Scripture: Numbers
13:1-3,25-33; 14:1-4,26-32;
20:1,2,7-12; 21:4-9

LESSON 28 FIRM FOUNDATIONS REVIEW SHEET

skit 28

Israel in the Promised Land under Judges and Kings

Readers: Uncle Don, Travis, Jessica

Travis:
I hate doing book reports.

Jessica:
Me, too. It's no fun.

Uncle Don:
I thought you kids liked to read.

Jessica:
We do—we just don't like to do book reports.

Uncle Don:
Maybe you just aren't clear about how to do a good report. What was your book about, Travis?

Travis:
It was a true story about a pioneer. He took his family across the country in a covered wagon, and then he built a house and settled down and cleared some land and started a farm.

Uncle Don:
Very good, Travis. What kind of man was he?

Travis:
Well, he was a hard worker, and he tried to finish everything he started, but it didn't always work out that way. And he liked to hunt and fish, and he loved his family.

Uncle Don:
If I were looking for a good pioneer story, I'd want to read that book. Good report, Travis.

Jessica:
Do you mean that was a book report?

Uncle Don:
It was a good start. Travis told us what the story was about and he also told us a lot about the main character. We can learn a lot from reading.

Jessica:
That was pretty easy. Let's try another book report.

Uncle Don:
I was hoping you would ask. How about the Bible!

Jessica:
But that's a great big book!

Uncle Don:
Yes, it is. But let's just ask the same questions and see what you've learned so far. What is the Bible all about?

Travis:
It's all about God and how He made everything and then He made man.

Jessica:
But then man sinned.

Travis:
But God made a way for man to come to him by faith. And He promised to send a Deliverer.

Uncle Don:
You're doing great!

Jessica:
Then men just refused to listen to God, so He sent a flood. But He rescued Noah and his whole family because they believed God.

Travis:
Then after the flood people did the same thing— they worshiped idols. But God called Abraham.

Jessica:
Abraham believed God.

Travis:
Abraham believed God, so God accepted him as if he were righteous. Abraham didn't have any children until he was 100 years old! But God promised a great nation through Abraham.

Jessica:
The nation was Israel! God rescued them lots of times—He even brought them across the sea on dry land and took care of them in the desert. They were always complaining. The Israelites never seemed to learn, but God was always faithful to keep His promises.

Uncle Don:
Great report, kids. Now, what about the main character of the Bible?

Travis:
God is the main character of the Bible, and He's perfect! He's holy!

Jessica:
And He loves us. But sin separated man from God.

Travis:
Only God can make a way for man to come to Him.

Jessica:
God knows everything, He's everywhere all the time, and He can do anything He wants—He's all powerful.

Uncle Don:
What do you think? Can you give a book report?

Travis:
I'm surprised. I didn't think we knew all that.

Uncle Don:
God gave the Bible so we could learn about Him. Most of the Old Testament tells how God worked through the Israelites. But the record was written for all of us, so we could know God. You kids have learned a lot. Let's learn some more!

Name _____

GOD

cared for Israel
in the Promised Land
and gave them
judges and kings

Use this WORD BANK to help you fill in the answers to the puzzle. When you have all the spaces filled, read the hidden message!

TEMPLE
DEATH
IDOLS
JUDGES
DEFEAT
SINNER
MERCY SEAT
GOD

Puzzle across: O K E P H I R O I S S

1. After Moses died, Joshua became the leader of Israel. _____ was Israel's true king, and He led the people through Joshua, just as He had led them through Moses.

2. After Joshua died, Israel turned away from the Lord. They began to worship _____.

3. Because Israel worshiped idols instead of worshiping God, God allowed their enemies to _____ them in battle.

4. When the Israelites would admit their sin to God, He raised up men and women called _____ to help them fight and overcome their enemies.

5. David was different from many of the kings who ruled Israel because he admitted that he was a _____. He trusted God to help Him.

6. God allowed David's son, Solomon, to build the _____ in Jerusalem. The temple was a permanent building to replace the tabernacle which the Israelites had built in the wilderness.

7. Every year the high priest would sacrifice a perfect animal for the sins of the people and would go in behind the curtain and sprinkle the blood on the _____ _____ . God would hold off for another year the punishment of the people's sins .

8. The blood of animals cannot pay for sin. The penalty for sin is the _____ of the sinner.

Lesson Scripture: Joshua 1:1,2;
11:23; Judges 2:7-19; II Samuel 5:4;
7:1-3,12-17; I Chronicles 22:5,6;
29:26-28; II Chronicles 2:1; 5:1

LESSON 29 FIRM FOUNDATIONS **REVIEW SHEET**

God's Prophets; Israel's Lack of Response

Readers: Uncle Don, Travis, Jessica

Uncle Don:
Travis, Jessica—what happened! I just saw the ambulance pull away as I came around the corner.

Travis:
It was awful, Uncle Don!

Jessica:
That new boy from down the street—he hit his head on the pavement.

Travis:
I think he might die! It could have been me!

Uncle Don:
Wait a minute, slow down! What happened?

Travis:
We were playing on our skateboards, and we started pulling each other. Then that boy's big brother came by in his car and said he'd tow us.

Uncle Don:
Oh, no! Your dad and mom have warned you and warned you about that.

Travis:
I know it. And their dad had just come by and warned us.

Jessica:
But the boy in the car said nobody would get hurt—he'd be real careful.

Travis:
So his little brother tried it first. Another car came around the corner just then and his brother swerved to miss him.

Jessica:
It was awful. He just flew off the skateboard and hit the bumper and then the pavement.

Travis:
I'm afraid he's going to die. Uncle Don, I'm so scared. I feel awful. I was going to try it next. It could have been me.

Uncle Don:
Travis, I hope you've learned a very important lesson. How many times were you told never to go behind a car on your skateboard?

Travis:
Too many times to count.

Jessica:
Travis, you could be dead right now.

Travis:
I know it. I feel terrible. And I feel so bad for that boy and his big brother.

Uncle Don:
It's **very** sad. When will you learn to listen to warnings? Travis, have you learned anything?

Travis:
I need to listen to what Dad and Mom tell me, no matter what anyone else says or does and no matter what I think I'd like to do.

Uncle Don:
That's exactly right. Travis, you are in **terrible danger** every time you refuse to heed a warning. There are many kinds of warnings . . .

Jessica:
Like tornado warnings and railroad crossing warnings . . .

Travis:
And warnings on medicine and on road signs.

Uncle Don:
Why do you think warnings are given?

Jessica:
To keep us from doing something that would harm us.

Travis:
To keep us out of trouble.

Uncle Don:
God gives us warnings, too. God warned Israel over and over, but the Israelites were just like you and your friends—they refused to listen.

Jessica:
What happened, Uncle Don?

Uncle Don:
God is very patient. Remember, He waited 120 years in the days of Noah before he sent the flood. Noah was warning the people during that time.

Travis:
They should have listened, just like me.

Uncle Don:
In the days of Israel's kings, the people were serving idols. God sent men called prophets to warn the Israelites to turn back to God or He would give them over to their enemies. But the people refused to listen, and they even killed some of God's prophets.

Travis:
Did they finally listen?

Uncle Don:
No, Travis. They didn't. They just kept on sinning. God did exactly what He had warned them He was going to do. It was a terrible time.

GOD Sent Prophets,
but Israel Refused to Respond

1. God sent special messengers called _____ to warn Israel to repent of their sins, destroy their idols, and trust only in Him.

2. God's prophets also told the people that God was going to send a _____ to save people from sin and Satan and death.

3. Most of the Israelites _____ to believe God; they persecuted and killed God's prophets, they worshiped idols, and they followed the evil ways of the nations around them.

4. They still offered sacrifices at the temple, but their _____ were far from God. God was (circle one)   PLEASED   NOT PLEASED with their worship and their sacrifices.

5. But God accepted all of those people who agreed with Him that they were _____ and trusted in Him for mercy and forgiveness.

6. God did exactly as He had _____. Because the Israelites refused to believe God's messages given through His prophets, God allowed the Assyrians to capture Israel and the Babylonians to capture Judah and to destroy Jerusalem.

7. After many years, the Lord brought some of the Israelites back to their land. They rebuilt the_____ in Jerusalem. The people were now called _____.

Use this word bank to fill in the answers to the questions above:

promised   refused   Jews   prophets   Deliverer   sinners   temple   hearts

Lesson Scripture: Isaiah 10:5,6;
Jeremiah 6:13,14; 20:5: II KIngs
17:1-8; 25:1-12

LESSON 30 FIRM FOUNDATIONS **REVIEW SHEET**

Uncle Don:
Well, kids, we've come to an exciting time in our Bible study!

Travis:
Did the Israelites finally listen to God?

Uncle Don:
No, not many of them ever did. But there were always a few people who believed God. The Israelites' enemies took them captive, but after many, many years God allowed them to return to their land.

Jessica:
Did they come back to Jerusalem?

Uncle Don:
Yes, they had to completely rebuild the city walls and rebuild the temple.

Travis:
Did they have a king then?

Uncle Don:
No, they were under foreign rulers—first the Persians, then Greeks and then the Romans.

Jessica:
When did all this happen?

Uncle Don:
The Israelites started coming back into their land aroud 500 B.C.

Travis:
Did God send them more prophets?

Uncle Don:
The last prophet during this time was Malachi. Then God did not give Israel any messages for about 400 years.

Travis:
Did anybody keep on believing God?

Uncle Don:
Just a few people. They knew God would do just as He had promised. They were eagerly awaiting the Deliverer whom God had promised to send. They actually thought God would send them a king to save them from the Roman rule.

Jessica:
So did God send them a king?

Uncle Don:
Not the kind of king they expected. No human being could really help them. God had promised a Deliverer who would deliver people from sin and Satan and death. All men have sinned. God cannot accept anything done by sinful man.

Travis:
What did God do?

Uncle Don:
God did the most amazing thing that has ever been done. He Himself came to be the Deliverer!

Jessica:
God came! I thought we couldn't see God.

Uncle Don:
That's right, Jessica. But remember? God is a Trinity—God the Father, God the Son, and God the Holy Spirit. God was going to send His own Son to be the Deliverer.

Travis:
It doesn't make sense.

Uncle Don:
What doesn't make sense, Travis?

Travis:
Well, it seems like all the people ever did was sin. They disobeyed God over and over. Why didn't God just wipe them all out?

Uncle Don:
He certainly could have, Travis. But He had promised to send a Deliverer. And there were always a few people who believed God. God is gracious and accepts those people who come to Him by faith, believing in Him to save them.

Jessica:
God is really patient, isn't He!

Uncle Don:
He really is, Jessica. And He knew exactly what was needed to save people from their sins. He knew that no one but He could do the job. It was an impossible thing for man to save himself, but **nothing is impossible to God.**

Travis:
But how could God come here as a man if He is God?

Uncle Don:
God performed a miracle. He caused His Son to be born to an ordinary woman. God the Son didn't have an earthly father. God was His Father. The Deliverer had to be sinless—He could not be related to Adam.

Travis:
Was it hard for God to come to earth?

Uncle Don:
God has all power—nothing is impossible to Him. But it must have been terribly hard to leave Heaven and come to such a sinful place. He did it because He loves us.

GOD Foretold the Birth of John and Jesus

Use this WORD BANK to help you fill in the answers to the questions below:
DELIVERER   JESUS   PREPARE THE WAY   GOD   SIN   GOD   ALL POWERFUL

1. John would be the one who would _____ _____ _____ for the Deliverer.

2. The Deliverer had to be born of a virgin so that He would not inherit Adam's _____.

3. Mary's son was to be given the name _____, which means "God saves" or "Saviour" or "Deliverer."

4. Jesus was fully man and fully _____. He truly was God, come down from Heaven.

5. Jesus could be given life without a human father because God is _____ _____. Nothing is impossible for God.

6. Jesus was to be the promised _____, whom God first promised in the Garden of Eden.

7. Who is the author of the New Testament? _____

Look up Luke 1:37 and write it here. Memorize this verse and write it from memory on the back of this sheet. _____

_____

God Began to Fulfill His Promises in John and Jesus

Readers: Uncle Don, Travis, Jessica

Travis:
Uncle Don, I have a question.

Uncle Don:
What's that, Travis?

Travis:
Well, today a lady came during our library hour and showed us a film on religions of the world. She had some great pictures. She told us that not everyone believes in the same kind of God.

Jessica:
But she said that was all right. She said that God accepts everyone, all around the world, just the same, any way they decide to come to Him.

Travis:
She said we are all God's children. Is that true?

Uncle Don:
Sounds very nice, doesn't it.

Travis:
Actually, it does. I really wanted to believe it, especially seeing all those good pictures.

Jessica:
But the Bible doesn't say that, does it?

Uncle Don:
No, kids, the Bible does not say that at all. As a matter of fact, the Bible says just the opposite. It says that all have sinned. Sin separates us from God. We are not "all God's children."

Travis:
And there is only one way to come to God, and that's God's way, not our way.

Uncle Don:
Travis, you are exactly right.

Jessica:
I don't know why, but the way she said it, I almost believed her. I **would have** believed her if we hadn't been having this Bible study!

Travis:
I hate to admit it, but I felt the same way.

Uncle Don:
This lady was no doubt sincere, but she was also sincerely wrong. She did not know the truth of God's Word. Probably without realizing it, she was speaking one of Satan's favorite lies.

Jessica:
Is that why it sounded so good?

Uncle Don:
I'm afraid so, Jessica. Remember, Satan shows himself like an angel of light sometimes.

Travis:
I really got confused just listening.

Uncle Don:
That's why it's so important to know exactly what the Bible says. God tells us in His Word that no one can come to God unless God makes a way for him to come. God is the only one who can deliver man from Satan and sin and death.

Jessica:
But what about all those people in other countries who have other religions?

Uncle Don:
Jessica, remember it was God who created all men. All of the people in the whole world were descended from the one man, Adam.

Travis:
So God knows about everyone. He hasn't made different ways for different people.

Uncle Don:
That's exactly right, Travis. He promised to send one Deliverer for the whole world. There is no other way anyone, anywhere can be saved.

Jessica:
But why are there so many religions?

Uncle Don:
Do you remember what happened after man sinned? Sin just increased on the earth. Do you remember what happened at the tower of Babel?

Travis:
God gave people all kinds of different languages.

Uncle Don:
People not only spoke different languages, they also had their own ideas. And besides that, Satan deceived them so that they worshiped the things which God created, instead of worshiping God, the Creator.

Jessica:
Uncle Don! I just remembered a verse we learned about Abraham! God said that **all nations** would be blessed through him.

Travis:
And the Deliverer was going to be his descendant!

Uncle Don:
Kids, you're right on target. One Saviour, for the whole world. God hasn't forgotten anyone. He has missionaries in places all over the world right now, telling people about His way of saving people from their sins!

GOD began to fulfill His promises about **John** and JESUS

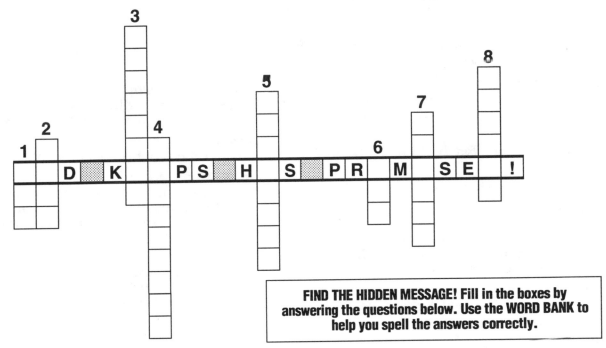

D K P S H S P R M S E !

FIND THE HIDDEN MESSAGE! Fill in the boxes by answering the questions below. Use the WORD BANK to help you spell the answers correctly.

1. The Bible was written down over the course of 1,600 years, by over 40 men. Every word of the Bible is true; every promise of the Bible is true. Who is the author of the Bible? _____

2. God gave Zacharias and Elizabeth a son in their old age. This son would be the one to prepare the way for the promised Deliverer. What was the name of their son? _____

3. God told Zacharias that the coming Deliverer or Saviour would fulfill all of God's _____ which He made to Abraham, Isaac, and Jacob, and through the prophets.

4. The promised Saviour would make a way for people to be _____ from their sins, from Satan, and from everlasting punishment.

5. Zacharias read and _____ what God had said in His Word through the prophets.

6. God was going to send just _____ Saviour (Deliverer) for the whole world.

7. Jesus, the promised Deliverer, would be God's greatest Prophet. He would also be the final great High _____, and King forever.

8. The Hebrew word, "Messiah," means _____.

WORD BANK			
ONE	PRIEST	PROMISES	CHRIST
GOD	JOHN	DELIVERED	BELIEVED

Jessica:
What a miserable day! It was supposed to be nice. Now we won't get to go to the park.

Travis:
I know. The weatherman predicted a perfect day—was he ever wrong!

Uncle Don:
Well, maybe we can do something here. I just happen to have things ready for an indoor picnic.

Jessica:
An indoor picnic? Really? That sounds great!

Travis:
Why not! I'm ready to eat!

Uncle Don:
By the way, don't be too hard on the weatherman. He has a lot of information available to him, but it's really impossible to know everything. Only God can do that.

Travis:
Do you mean that God knew it would be like this today?

Uncle Don:
Sure He did, Travis. God knows everything. That's one of the truly amazing things about the Bible.

Jessica:
What's that?

Uncle Don:
God gave men prophesies to write down hundreds of years before the things actually came to pass. Some of the prophecies were given several **thousand** years before the things God mentioned actually happened.

Travis:
Thousands of years? That **is** amazing!

Uncle Don:
And what is even more amazing is that every single one of these prophecies either has been fulfilled or will yet be fulfilled. And every detail will be fulfilled exactly as God said it would be.

Travis:
Somehow, that's hard to imagine.

Uncle Don:
It really is, Travis. It would be kind of the same as if someone over a thousand years ago wrote down some of the things about **your** life, exactly as they were to happen.

Jessica:
What kinds of things?

Uncle Don:
I'm thinking of the kinds of things that the prophets wrote about Jesus—where He would be born, where His parents would have to move to, and where they would return to live when Jesus was growing up.

Travis:
Like if someone wrote what city I'd be born in, and that later on we'd move right here next to you!

Uncle Don:
That's exactly right, Travis. That's the kind of things that were written down by God's prophets hundreds of years before Jesus was born.

Jessica:
How did the prophets know what to write?

Uncle Don:
That's what makes prophecy so special—it is really the words of God, communicated into the mind of the prophet, who then wrote down God's exact messages.

Travis:
So the prophets were really writing down exactly what God told them to write, and that's why the prophecies came true.

Uncle Don:
That's right, Travis. God had His prophets write down hundreds of prophecies about the coming Deliverer.

Jessica:
Why did God do that?

Uncle Don:
He wanted people to know when the Deliverer came. He would fulfill the exact words written about Him. These words were for us, today, too, so we could know that Jesus is the promised Deliverer. Imagine! God actually came to earth!

Travis:
Did people back then realize who He was?

Uncle Don:
Only a few people did. Think about it: the little baby placed in an animal food trough was really the Son of God!

Jessica:
Oh, Uncle Don, that's just too amazing!

Travis:
Did Mary and Joseph understand who He was?

Uncle Don:
God told them through His angel, but it must have been hard even for them to realize that this baby boy was really Emmanuel—God with us!

GOD fulfilled His promises by giving
JESUS, the Deliverer

**FILL IN THE BLANKS using this WORD BANK
to help you:**

Bethlehem   Egypt   Adam's   Israel   Deliverer   wrong
God With Us   God   God the Son

1. The name Emmanuel means, "_____ _____ _____."

2. Jesus was born in the country of _____.

3. The prophets had written that Jesus would be born in the town of _____.

4. It was right for the wise men to worship Jesus, because Jesus was _____ ____ _____.

5. God told Joseph to take Jesus to _____ in order to escape from Herod.

6. Jesus, God the Son, was born into the world to be the _____ of sinners—to save people from Satan and sin and death.

7. Jesus looked like other children, but He was different in that He was truly _____ as well as being human.

8. Jesus never did anything _____ , that is, He never sinned. He was born sinless, and he never thought, said, or did anything which displeased God.

9. Only Jesus was born sinless; everyone else inherited _____ nature to sin.

Travis:
Uncle Don, I wonder what I'll be when I grow up.

Uncle Don:
That's a good question, Travis. I know of someone who knows the answer!

Jessica:
God knows, doesn't He!

Uncle Don:
He sure does, Jessica. Do you remember the words Zecharias spoke about his son, John? God the Holy Spirit told Zecharias that John would be the one to prepare the way for the Deliverer.

Travis:
God knew even before John was born!

Uncle Don:
It was the same with Jesus Christ, God's own Son. God sent Him to be the Deliverer. God planned it all before He created the earth! He knew we would need a Saviour.

Jessica:
God is just amazing! I can't understand all that!

Uncle Don:
I can't either, but I believe it.

Travis:
What did God mean when He said that John would prepare the way for the Deliverer?

Uncle Don:
The Deliverer, Jesus Christ, came to earth to save people from their sins. God wanted people to realize that they were sinners, needing a Saviour.

Jessica:
Do you mean that people didn't know that?

Uncle Don:
Jessica, I can remember a time when you didn't think you had ever broken any of God's commandments.

Jessica:
You're right, Uncle Don. I forgot about that. I really didn't think I had. But I sure know it now.

Travis:
How did John get people to think about their sins?

Uncle Don:
John went out in the countryside and preached to the people. He told them they must repent, because the kingdom of God was near.

Jessica:
What does repent mean?

Uncle Don:
To repent means to change your mind about yourself and your sin and to see yourself as a sinner. To repent means to agree with God that you are a sinner, needing a Saviour.

Travis:
I thought it meant that a person should feel bad about what they've done and never do it again.

Uncle Don:
A lot of people think that's what it means, but really, God wants people to come to Him just as they are, as sinners. Only God can save people from their sins.

Jessica:
What did John mean when he said that the kingdom of Heaven was near?

Uncle Don:
He was announcing the fact that Jesus, the Deliverer, had come to earth.

Travis:
Did the people understand what he meant?

Uncle Don:
Not really. But a few people who were looking for the Deliverer started to follow Jesus and learn from Him. They weren't totally able to understand that He was really God. They were expecting a king who would deliver them from the Romans.

Jessica:
John had a really special job—telling people that Jesus was coming!

Uncle Don:
He really did, Jessica. But you know something? John was a very poor man. He lived out in the wilderness and ate the food he could find there.

Travis:
That's amazing. I figured he'd be really rich. After all, He was doing a big job for God.

Uncle Don:
No, Travis, that isn't God's way. That is man's way. John was rich toward God—He believed God, and God accepted him. But in the world's eyes John was very poor. So was Jesus.

Travis:
God is just so surprising. He's not like I thought.

Jessica:
He's . . . well, He's better. He always does everything so special.

Uncle Don:
Jessica, you're so right. God is wonderful!

GOD sent John to teach and baptize; John baptized JESUS

1. John told the people to _____ and be baptized.

2. To repent means to _____ _____ _____ about ourselves, our sin, and God—to agree with God that we are sinners, unable to make ourselves acceptable to God.

3. The _____ were Jewish religious leaders who made the hand-written copies of the Old Testament on scrolls. They were very proud of what they knew about God's Word, and they thought that their knowledge would make them acceptable to God.

4. The _____ were Jewish religious leaders who had added many rules to God's laws. They were very proud of themselves and thought God should accept them because they did so many "good deeds."

5. The _____ were Jewish religious leaders who did not accept all of God's Word. They were more interested in pleasing the Roman rulers than they were in pleasing God.

6. Does getting baptized save us from our sins?   YES   NO

7. "Deliverer," "Saviour," and "Emmanuel," are some of the names of _____ _____.

8. When Jesus came up out of the water after being baptized, God spoke from Heaven and said that Jesus was His beloved _____ . God was completely pleased with Him.

9. John called Jesus the _____ _____ _____ .

Jesus, When Tempted, Resisted and Rebuked Satan

Readers: Uncle Don, Travis, Jessica

Uncle Don:
Hi, kids. What's going on?

Jessica:
It's Travis! He saw another one of those scary movies at his friend's house yesterday. I hate it when he tells me about that creepy stuff.

Travis:
It was neat! There was this guy who had a spaceship, and he got in a battle with an evil force. It was scary!

Jessica:
I don't want to hear any more about it! Mom has told you a hundred times not to watch that stuff.

Uncle Don:
Your mom is right. Travis, those movies are a bunch of lies. But there is a real enemy and we need to know the truth about him.

Travis:
Do you mean Satan?

Uncle Don:
Yes.

Jessica:
We studied about him before. He was one of God's created angels, but he rebelled against God.

Travis:
And he lost his place of service in Heaven.

Jessica:
And one day God is going to throw him and his followers into the Lake of Fire!

Uncle Don:
You kids have really learned a lot. We need to know about this terrible enemy of God and man, and the Bible is the only place that gives us the truth.

Jessica:
What did Satan do when Jesus came to earth?

Uncle Don:
That's exactly what I wanted to tell you about, Jessica. Satan tried to do to Jesus just the same thing as Satan did to Adam and Eve in the garden—he tried to make Jesus sin.

Travis:
Did he come to Him like a snake?

Uncle Don:
No, there was no way he could hide his identity from Jesus. Jesus knows everything!

Jessica:
So what happened?

Uncle Don:
The Bible tells us that God the Holy Spirit led Jesus into the wilderness and Jesus spent forty days without eating.

Travis:
Why would God do that?

Uncle Don:
Well, the Bible doesn't tell us exactly. But we can learn quite a bit from what we **are** told. Jesus was allowing Himself to be tempted in the same way that ordinary men are tempted.

Travis:
What do you mean?

Uncle Don:
You can imagine that after not eating, Jesus was very, very hungry and tired. By becoming a man, Jesus had given up the privileges He had in Heaven. He allowed Himself to be weak and needy, just like other men.

Jessica:
I never knew that! Why would He do that?

Uncle Don:
He wanted to go through all the hard things we go through, so we would know that He understands us. And He wanted to go through everything we go through but fully obey God. Jesus went through temptation, but He never sinned once.

Travis:
You mean He **always** obeyed God, no matter what?

Uncle Don:
That's right, Travis. Satan even tried to get Jesus to perform a miracle and make the rocks in the desert turn into bread.

Jessica:
Jesus could have done that if He had wanted to! He is God!

Uncle Don:
You're absolutely right, Jessica. But He refused to do it, because God never told Him to do it.

Travis:
Did Jesus do any big miracles out there in the desert when Satan came to tempt Him?

Uncle Don:
Jesus did something no man has ever been able to do. He completely resisted Satan and completely obeyed God. Jesus is greater than Satan—Jesus Christ is God! God is superior to Satan in every way. Even as a man, a very hungry, tired man, Jesus defeated Satan. And He did it by using God's Word.

Name _____

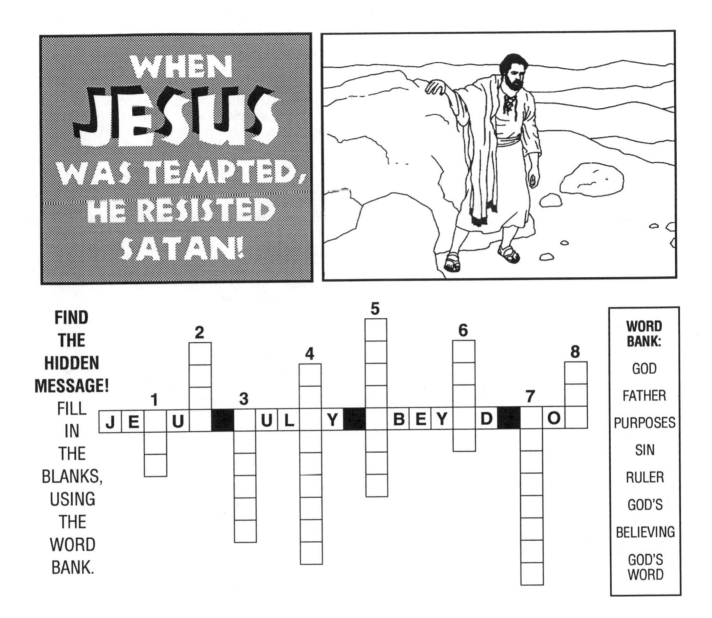

WHEN JESUS WAS TEMPTED, HE RESISTED SATAN!

FIND THE HIDDEN MESSAGE! FILL IN THE BLANKS, USING THE WORD BANK.

```
                    2        4      5        6            8
         1       3                              7
   J E _ U _ _ _ U L _ Y _ B E Y _ D _ _ O
```

WORD BANK:
GOD
FATHER
PURPOSES
SIN
RULER
GOD'S
BELIEVING
GOD'S WORD

1. Satan tempted Jesus because Satan wanted Jesus to ____ so that Jesus could not be our Deliverer.

2. Satan tried to make Jesus worship him. Satan wanted to take _____ position.

3. Jesus refused to turn the stones into bread because His _____ did not tell Him to do this. Jesus would do only those things His Father told Him to do.

4. Knowing and _____ God's Word is more important than having food to eat.

5. Satan knows God's Word, but he twists it for his own evil _____.

6. Satan could offer Jesus the position of _____ over all the world because when Adam obeyed Satan, Satan became the ruler over Adam and all the human race.

7. Jesus fought against Satan by using _____ _____.

8. Jesus is greater than Satan. Jesus is _____, the One who created Lucifer (Satan), who rebelled against Him. One day, Jesus will throw Satan into the Lake of Fire.

Lesson Scripture: Matthew 4:1-11   **LESSON 35**   **Firm FOUNDATIONS REVIEW SHEET**

Jesus Began His Ministry

Readers: Uncle Don, Travis, Jessica

Travis:
You know, Uncle Don, I'm beginning to see that Jesus was different from what I thought.

Uncle Don:
In what way, Travis?

Travis:
Well, I never could think of Him as a real man. I just saw Bible pictures and thought about the stories, but He didn't seem real.

Uncle Don:
So how do you think of Him now?

Travis:
I'm not sure. He just seems so powerful, but like a real person.

Jessica:
I didn't realize He got tired and hungry!

Travis:
It's just hard to imagine—how He was really God and yet He was a real man.

Uncle Don:
But that's exactly who He was—truly God and truly man.

Jessica:
I'd sure love to have been there to see Him!

Uncle Don:
Me, too, Jessica. A lot of people came to listen to Him teach. He really surprised them because He taught God's Word clearly and with power.

Travis:
I'll bet they liked to listen to Him!

Uncle Don:
Yes, people came from everywhere to hear Him. Unfortunately, the religious teachers of the Jews were not clearly teaching God's Word, so Jesus' messages were very refreshing to the people.

Jessica:
How old was He?

Uncle Don:
He was about thirty years old when He began His ministry.

Travis:
I think that's about how old Dad is!

Uncle Don:
Jesus was very popular with the people. And He amazed them because He had the power to cast out demons. Pretty soon everyone was talking about Jesus.

Jessica:
What are demons?

Uncle Don:
Demons are the spirits who joined in Satan's rebellion against God. Demons follow Satan. They hate God and like to live in and control people who are the children of Satan.

Travis:
How did Jesus cast them out?

Uncle Don:
He just spoke to them, and they had to leave the person they were tormenting. Jesus is stronger than Satan and all of his demons. The demons had to obey Jesus.

Travis:
Jesus really is strong!

Jessica:
There's no one like Jesus!

Uncle Don:
You're right, Jessica! Many people began to follow Him. Jesus was preaching the Good News everywhere He went.

Travis:
What Good News?

Uncle Don:
The Good News that the kingdom of God was near. Jesus was God Himself. He had come to deliver people from Satan and sin and death.

Jessica:
I'll bet people were excited!

Uncle Don:
They didn't necessarily understand who He was, but it was hard to miss the things He did.

Travis:
What kind of things?

Uncle Don:
He healed people everywhere He went. He even healed a man who was sick with leprosy.

Jessica:
What's leprosy?

Uncle Don:
Leprosy is a disease that kills the nerves and may cause a person to lose a hand or foot or even his nose. No one would **dare** to touch a leper.

Jessica:
That sounds awful! How did Jesus heal him?

Uncle Don:
Jesus **touched** the man. There's no one as powerful or as kind as Jesus!

JESUS Began His Ministry

Word Bank: God   sinners   rebelled   believe   sin
proud   disciples   authority   servants

1. The Pharisees and other religious leaders refused to accept the teaching of John the Baptist. Their attitudes were _____. They thought that they were "good enough" for God to accept them. (A person who is proud thinks that he is better than others. A proud person thinks that he does not need God's help.)

2. Jesus told the people that they must repent, that is, they must change their minds about their sin and about God. They must agree with God that they were helpless_____, and they must believe the Good News Jesus came to tell them.

3. The only way that a person can please God is to _____ His Word.

4. Jesus called several men to be His _____, or followers. Some of these men were fishermen.

5. Jesus taught with _____. He knew and understood what God said in His Word. The scribes and Pharisees just gave their own opinions about what they thought God meant.

6. The demons were originally created as God's _____—angels who lived in Heaven with God. But when they followed Lucifer and _____ against God, God removed them from their places of service in Heaven.

7. The demons were afraid of Jesus. They knew that He was _____, and they knew that one day, He would throw them and all who follow Satan into the Lake of Fire.

8. Leprosy reminds us of _____, because no ordinary person could cure someone of leprosy. Jesus cured the man of leprosy. In the same way, only God can deliver us from the power and the punishment of our sins.

Lesson Scripture: Mark 1:14-28, 34-42   **LESSON 36**   FIRM FOUNDATIONS   **REVIEW SHEET**   © New Tribes Mission, 1993   Permission given to photocopy for classroom use

You Must Be Born Again

Readers: Uncle Don, Travis, Jessica

Uncle Don:
Well, Travis, that was a nice birthday party!

Travis:
I liked the cake Mom made!

Jessica:
You always like cake! When is **your** birthday, Uncle Don?

Uncle Don:
Which one?

Jessica:
What do you mean, "which one"?

Uncle Don:
Well, Jessica, I have two birthdays. The first one was when I was born as a little baby. Everybody has that kind of a birthday.

Travis:
But what is the second birthday all about?

Uncle Don:
Travis, do you remember what happened in the Garden of Eden?

Travis:
Adam and Eve sinned.

Uncle Don:
Yes. And the sad thing is that every person born since then is a sinner—a descendant of Adam.

Travis:
But we can't do anything about how we're born!

Uncle Don:
You're right, we can't. But God has made a way for us to be born a second time—not related to Adam, but related to God!

Jessica:
Really?

Uncle Don:
That's right, Jessica. God knows that we can't do anything to change the way we are. We have inherited Adam's sinful nature. And so, no matter how hard we try, we are unable to change ourselves so that we can obey God and please Him.

Travis:
But what about that preacher we met the other day. Can't he obey and please God?

Uncle Don:
Not if he's depending on his own strength and has never been born again. No one can live to please God unless he has first been born again by putting his trust in Jesus Christ as his Saviour.

Jessica:
Born again? But I thought you could only be born once!

Uncle Don:
Actually, it was Jesus Himself who talked about being born again. He was talking to Nicodemus, one of the Jewish religious leaders.

Travis:
But that sounds really strange. How can a person be born again?

Uncle Don:
In the same way that I was born again—I believed in Jesus Christ as my Saviour. When I did that, I was born again into God's family.

Travis:
What do you mean, "into God's family"?

Uncle Don:
Adam and Eve were separated from God. Their disobedience put them and all their descendants out of God's family and into Satan's family.

Jessica:
But what about God's family?

Uncle Don:
A person can be born into God's family by believing in Jesus Christ. That's the only way to be born a second time.

Travis:
Who can get born again?

Uncle Don:
The only people who can be born again are sinners! Everyone is a sinner by birth. All that God asks is that a person admit that he is a hopeless sinner, unable to save himself. The moment that person puts his faith in Jesus Christ as his Saviour, he is born again.

Travis:
Is that how you were born again?

Uncle Don:
Yes. I just admitted to God that I was a sinner, unable to do anything to take care of my sins. I believed that Jesus was the only Saviour, the only one who could deliver me from sin and Satan and death.

Jessica:
So do you really have two birthdays?

Uncle Don:
I sure do, Jessica, and the second one is the best. The Bible says that whoever believes in Jesus Christ will have everlasting life! What a birthday present!

Name _____

YOU MUST BE BORN AGAIN

WORD BANK: Holy Spirit   good works   God's Word   believes   miracles   Abraham

1. Nicodemus believed that Jesus was sent by God because Nicodemus saw the _____ that Jesus did.

2. The Pharisees were trusting in their _____ _____ to get them to Heaven. They also thought that God would accept them because they were descendants of _____.

3. Jesus said that we must be born again. We must hear, understand, and believe _____ _____.

4. God the _____ _____ uses God's Word to cause us to be born into God's family.

5. Jesus came to be our Deliverer from Satan and sin and death. God saves whoever _____ in Jesus Christ.

☞ GOOD NEWS FOR EVERYONE ☜ IN THE WHOLE WORLD!

In your Bible Look up John 3:16 and write it on the lines below. Then memorize it!

_____

_____

_____

_____

_____

Lesson Scripture: John 3:1-7,14-20   **LESSON 37** FIRM FOUNDATIONS **REVIEW SHEET**   © New Tribes Mission, 1993

Permission given to photocopy for classroom use

Uncle Don:
Hi, Jessica. How are you today?

Jessica:
Fine! Did you know that Jimmy wants to come over and study the Bible with us?

Uncle Don:
Hey, that's great! When is he coming?

Travis:
Well, I don't know if he can really come.

Uncle Don:
Why is that?

Travis:
Well, his dad wasn't too happy about it.

Jessica:
He said that religious people are a bunch of hippo—something?

Uncle Don:
Did he say "hypocrite"?

Travis:
That's it! Hypocrites—that was the word he used.

Jessica:
What does "hypocrites" mean?

Uncle Don:
A hypocrite is a person who pretends on the outside to be very religious; but on the inside he really doesn't believe God. He doesn't see himself as a sinner, as God sees him.

Travis:
Everybody has sinned.

Uncle Don:
That's right, Travis. And Jimmy's dad has probably been disappointed by the way someone acted. He may even have looked up to some person as being very "religious" in his eyes—he may have never expected them to sin. Then when that person sinned, Jimmy's dad may have gotten bitter against God because of what the person did.

Jessica:
Jimmy's dad shouldn't care about how other people act—he does a lot of bad things! You should have seen what he . . .

Uncle Don:
Jessica, **Jesus came to save sinners! All of us are sinners**. Sin isn't just the outward things. It's the things in our hearts, like anger and pride and jealousy. Jimmy's dad needs to know that God is not like those people who are calling themselves religious. That's why Jesus was loved so much by some of the sinners with whom He came in contact.

Travis:
What do you mean, Uncle Don?

Uncle Don:
Well, Jesus was **always** godly. He wasn't covering up any sin inside of Him. He was completely good—as a matter of fact, He **never** sinned.

Jessica:
You mean that people never once saw Him do anything bad?

Uncle Don:
That's right, Jessica. Jesus only did those things that pleased God. He never had to worry about being a hypocrite. What He was on the outside was exactly what He was on the inside.

Travis:
Man, how did He live like that?

Uncle Don:
Jesus is God. When the people came to Him, He always did and said the things God told Him to.

Travis:
I'll bet Jimmy's dad would be impressed with someone like Jesus!

Uncle Don:
I hope that He would! In Jesus' time here on earth, many people like Jimmy's dad did put their trust in Jesus. But other people rejected Jesus.

Jessica:
Rejected Him? Why would anyone do that?

Uncle Don:
For the very reason we were just talking about. Some people were hypocrites, that is, they did not care as much about God as they cared about themselves and making an impression on other people. The Pharisees were like that.

Travis:
Man, things weren't a lot different back when Jesus came to earth—the people who upset Jimmy's dad are kind of like modern-day Pharisees, aren't they?

Uncle Don:
I'm afraid so, Travis. Jesus spoke out very harshly against the Pharisees. God is looking at men's hearts, and He is never fooled by what people say or do. He knows every one of us, exactly as we are.

JESUS showed that He is truly GOD

JESUS chose twelve men to be His disciples

WORD BANK:	SINNERS
GOD AUTHORITY	DISCIPLES
TAX COLLECTOR	HYPOCRITE
FISHERMEN	JEALOUS

1. Because Jesus is _____ He had the _____ to forgive the paralyzed man's sins and to heal him.

2. Levi was a _____ _____ when Jesus called him.

3. Jesus came to call and to save _____ .

4. If a person does a lot of good works, can he expect God to accept him in Heaven?

   YES   NO

5. Many of the scribes and the Pharisees hated Jesus and wanted to find a way to have Him killed. They were _____ of Him. They did not believe that He was God.

6. A person who acts religious on the outside but is really living a sinful life is called a _____ .

7. Most of the men whom Jesus chose to be His followers or _____ were not wealthy or well-educated. They were just ordinary men. Many of them were _____ .

Travis:
Uncle Don, I was really surprised how well you got along with Jimmy's dad, Mr. Johnson!

Uncle Don:
You know, Travis, I was surprised, too. I'm really glad he's decided to let Jimmy come over and study the Bible with us.

Jessica:
After all he said about religion and hypocrites, I couldn't believe he'd let Jimmy come.

Uncle Don:
I don't know if anyone had ever asked him about just studying the Bible. You have to remember that he really does care about Jimmy.

Travis:
I guess I saw a different side of him when you were talking to him. All I ever noticed was him yelling at Jimmy and getting another cigarette or a drink.

Uncle Don:
Mr. Johnson is a very unhappy man, even though he has a lot of money. I guess he owns more than anyone in this neighborhood, but he doesn't have any peace of mind.

Jessica:
Have you seen Jimmy's older brother, Eddie?

Travis:
He's **really** strange! I won't go near him!

Uncle Don:
Sad to say, but that's best. That boy has gotten into some deep trouble. I don't want either of you to be with him. That's one reason I'd like to have Jimmy visit over here—so you won't go over to Johnsons and run into Eddie.

Jessica:
I saw him in a store a couple of months ago. He'd scare anybody. He looks wild.

Travis:
I heard that he takes lots of drugs.

Jessica:
He's been in jail a lot, but Mr. Johnson gets him out. He doesn't live at home though. They don't get along.

Travis:
Jimmy said that Eddie is in another program now, whatever that means.

Uncle Don:
Oh, they're trying to help him get straightened out. He ran away from the last program.

Jessica:
Mrs. Davis down the street said there's no hope for Eddie. He's just a crazy man.

Uncle Don:
I know what she meant—and she's right as far as what men can do—no person, no program, can change Eddie. But he **can** be changed!

Travis:
How?

Uncle Don:
In the same way that God has made for you and me to be forgiven and cleansed from our sins. Do you remember what Jesus told Nicodemus?

Travis:
He told him he had to be born again!

Jessica:
But isn't Eddie's problem a lot worse? Doesn't he need something more?

Uncle Don:
Jessica, sin is sin. It all costs the same penalty: death. Jesus Christ is the **only** one who can help sinners. There's no other answer for you or for me or for Eddie or for anyone else in the whole world.

Travis:
I hate to say it, but has Jesus ever been able to help anybody as bad as Eddie?

Uncle Don:
He certainly has! Jesus is God. **Nothing** is too hard for Him. The Bible gives us some wonderful, true stories of people very much like Eddie who were totally changed by Jesus.

Jessica:
But that was back then, when Jesus was on the earth as a man. What about today?

Uncle Don:
Jesus hasn't changed. He is still giving new life to people who put their faith in Him. Do you remember Betty, the missionary we met last week? At one time, she was a lot like Eddie.

Travis:
You're kidding!

Uncle Don:
No, as a matter of fact, she said that her story was a lot like the story of the man of Gadara in the Bible. At one time, Betty was totally in bondage to Satan, but Jesus set her free. Let's look at the Bible story in Mark 5.

JESUS calmed the storm and delivered a demon-possessed man

WORD BANK:
afraid   Jesus   man   God   created

1. Jesus is truly God. But when He came to earth as a _____, He experienced the things that all of us experience: He got tired and hungry, and He needed sleep.

2. The disciples were very _____ of the storm, but God was watching over them.

3. Jesus could command the wind and the sea to be quiet because Jesus is _____. He _____ the air and the water.

4. Could the demon-possessed man deliver himself from the power of the demons?   YES   NO

5. Is any one of us strong enough to deliver a person from Satan?   YES   NO

6. _____ is the only one who can deliver all people from the power of Satan and sin and death.

BONUS: Unscramble the letters to find what is too hard for Jesus to do: _____!
G T O H N N I

LESSON 39 Firm **FOUNDATIONS** **REVIEW SHEET**

Travis:
Man, this corn on the cob is great!

Jessica:
I like the fried chicken best of all.

Travis:
And the potato salad!

Jimmy:
I like it all!

Travis:
Me, too. May I have some more chicken, please?

Uncle Don:
Sure, Travis. I'm glad you kids are enjoying our picnic. I thought it was a good day for it. We can have our regular Bible study when we're finished eating.

Jimmy:
I'm sure glad you invited me to come, too! This is great!

Uncle Don:
Jimmy, we are really glad to have you with us. Travis, you may want to leave room for some dessert!

Travis:
Dessert! Wow! Why didn't you tell me—I'm stuffed!

Jessica:
Give him five minutes, Uncle Don. He'll be ready.

Travis:
What kind of dessert is it?

Uncle Don:
Nothing special. Just some brownies and ice cream.

Travis:
I'm ready!

Jessica:
See, I told you.

Uncle Don:
Jimmy, you're not eating much.

Jimmy:
Oh, I was just thinking about something.

Uncle Don:
Do you want to tell us about it?

Jimmy:
Well, I was thinking about my dad and my brother Eddie. They just don't know how much fun something like this can be.

Uncle Don:
Something like what, Jimmy? You mean all the food?

Jimmy:
Oh, not that. I mean, well, the food is great, and I'm having a good time with you all. But I was talking about our Bible study.

Jessica:
The Bible study?

Jimmy:
I never knew how many neat things are in the Bible. I never knew about Jesus Christ. I think my dad and Eddie would like Jesus, too, if they would only listen.

Uncle Don:
Well, Jimmy, they may just do that one day. Your good attitude just may make them want to know what it is that you are enjoying so much! Here, do you want another brownie?

Jimmy:
No thanks, Uncle Don. When can we start our Bible study?

Uncle Don:
As soon as we get the table cleared off and can roll Travis into a more comfortable position. He looks a little overstuffed.

Travis:
I am. But it was **so** good!

Jessica:
Travis, you made a pig of yourself!

Travis:
You're right—I think I kind of overdid it.

Uncle Don:
Do you know something—there's one thing you can eat and eat and enjoy more and more and never eat too much! The problem is, many people don't seem to think they have any appetite for it.

Jessica:
What are you talking about?

Uncle Don:
I'm talking about God's Word. I think Jimmy is one of those people who has a taste for it. Most of the people in Jesus' time were just like most people now. They would rather have food for their stomachs than something to satisfy their hearts. Jimmy, you're on the right track when you are thirsty and hungry to know more about God.

Name _____

JESUS fed 5,000 people!

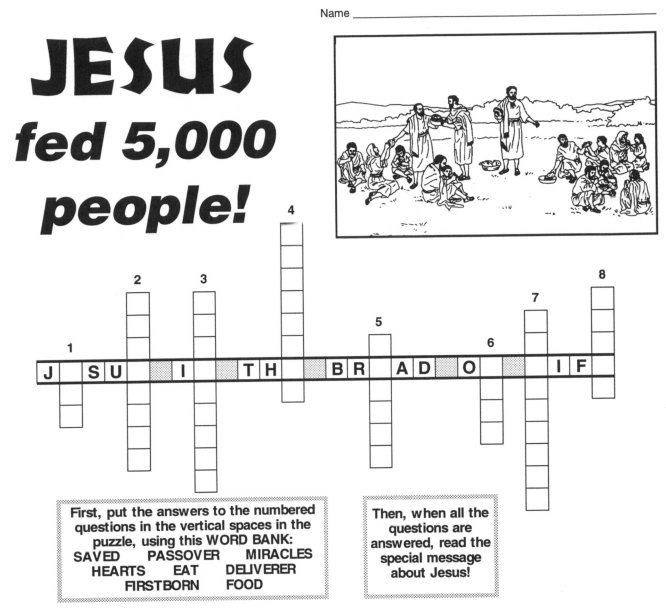

Crossword puzzle with answer row:

J S U _ I _ T H _ B R _ A D _ O _ _ I F

First, put the answers to the numbered questions in the vertical spaces in the puzzle, using this WORD BANK:
SAVED   PASSOVER   MIRACLES
HEARTS   EAT   DELIVERER
FIRSTBORN   FOOD

Then, when all the questions are answered, read the special message about Jesus!

1. The people were following Jesus because He had given them something to _____ .

2. The Jews celebrated the _____ feast in remembrance of God's great deliverance of the Israelites from the Egyptians.

3. When God saw the blood on their doorposts, He passed over their houses and none of their _____ died.

4. Jesus performed great _____, showing that He truly is God.

5. Jesus would not allow the people to make Him king, because He knew that in their _____ they only wanted someone to deliver them from the Romans.

6. The people cared more about _____ for their bodies than they cared about the wonderful, everlasting life Jesus wanted to give them.

7. God gave the Israelites manna in the wilderness so they would not die. In the same way, God sent Jesus Christ to be the great _____ so that people would not have to go to everlasting punishment.

8. Everyone who trusts only in Jesus is _____ from Satan, sin, and everlasting punishment.

Lesson Scripture: John 6:1-35   **LESSON 40** FIRM FOUNDATIONS **REVIEW SHEET**

The Way of the Scribes and Pharisees Is Not God's Way

Readers: Uncle Don, Travis, Jessica

Jessica:
Did you hear those boys talking at recess?

Travis:
I sure did! That was awful!

Jessica:
Our dad would never stand for that. I'm sure glad I don't talk like they do. Did you know that I'm learning Bible verses?

Travis:
I think you told me a couple of times.

Jessica:
Oh. Did I? Well, anyway, if I can learn another ten verses I'll have **fifty** verses memorized!

Travis:
So?

Jessica:
So, I think that's pretty good!

Travis:
I guess so.

Jessica:
You **guess** so?!

Travis:
Well, it's just that you sound so proud of yourself.

Jessica:
I have a right to be proud of myself. It takes a lot of time to learn verses.

Travis:
I learned to say the alphabet backwards once, but I think I forgot it now.

Jessica:
Learning the alphabet is nothing to be proud of. But learning verses is really something God is pleased with.

Oh, hi, Uncle Don.

Uncle Don:
Hi, Jessica. Hello, Travis.

Jessica:
Isn't that right, Uncle Don—learning Bible verses really pleases God—a lot more than learning the alphabet pleases Him!

Uncle Don:
This sounds like an interesting conversation. Who is learning Bible verses?

Jessica:
I am. I have forty memorized already.

Uncle Don:
Really. What are you learning now?

Jessica:
I Samuel 16:7: ". . . man looketh on the outward appearance, but the LORD looketh on the heart."

Uncle Don:
Very good. Do you know what that means?

Jessica:
Not really.

Uncle Don:
Have you ever been turned off by someone because of something they said or did or how they looked?

Jessica:
Yes! Travis and I heard some boys at recess. They were awful. I'd **never** talk like they did.

Uncle Don:
You and Travis have both been taught well at home. I wonder if those boys are as fortunate.

Jessica:
What do you mean?

Uncle Don:
Did you ever stop to think about why people act like they act?

Travis:
Like Jessica. She acts like she thinks she's important because she's memorized some verses.

Jessica:
Travis!

Uncle Don:
Kids! Let's think about this. To learn verses is excellent. God wants us to know His Word. But to be proud of yourself **isn't** good. Remember? God's Word tells us that we are **all** sinners, just like those boys. You were very aware of their sins because of what they said; but did you have a right attitude in your heart about them and about yourselves? I think you were looking down on them and putting yourselves on a pedestal. Even if a person learned the whole Bible—having done that still wouldn't take care of his sins. Jessica, did you know that pride is sin?

Jessica:
Uncle Don, you're right. When God looks at my heart, He sees that I'm a sinner, even if I do memorize verses.

Uncle Don:
Very true, Jessica. Jesus had a lot to say about all this—people back in New Testament times were like us. Travis, you and I need this, too. Let's look in our Bibles at Mark 7.

Name _____

The Way of the **Scribes** and **Pharisees** Is Not God's Way

Use this WORD BANK to fill in the answers :	sins	hearts	mercy	lips	proud	rules	agreed	hearts

1. The Pharisees were angry with Jesus' disciples because the disciples did not follow all the
   _____ which the Pharisees claimed were necessary to please God.

2. The prophet Isaiah said that people like the Pharisees honored God with their _____
   but their _____ were far from God.

3. People judge other people by what they think they see on the outside, but God looks at our
   _____ .

4. God accepted the tax collector because this man _____ with God about his
   _____ . He knew he was a sinner who needed God's _____ .

5. The Pharisee was _____ of himself. He thought God would accept him because
   of his own goodness. Did God accept him?   YES   NO

- -

PUT THESE WORDS WITH THE RIGHT MAN:
(One of these words goes with both men!)
repentant   proud
sinful   trusted God
trusted self

PHARISEE	TAX COLLECTOR
_____	_____
_____	_____
_____	_____

Lesson Scripture: Mark 7:1-9; 14-23;
Luke 18:9-14

LESSON 41 FIRM FOUNDATIONS **REVIEW SHEET**

Jessica:
My cousin Mary is home from college this week. She's staying at our house, and I get to share my room with her!

Uncle Don:
Are you having a good time together?

Jessica:
It's lots of fun! She has some neat music and she let me use some of her makeup.

Uncle Don:
I wondered what had happened to you!

Jessica:
I kind of put on too much, didn't I?

Uncle Don:
So what else are you doing with Mary?

Jessica:
We went shopping together. Mom took us to the mall, and we bought a lot of stuff. Then we came home and made some cookies. Mom said Mary could take some back to college with her. But we ate a lot, too!

Uncle Don:
Sounds like you're having fun.

Jessica:
Well, kind of.

Uncle Don:
Now, what does that mean?

Jessica:
I don't know how to say it—remember what we read about the Pharisee?

Uncle Don:
I sure do.

Jessica:
Well, it's not quite the same, but Mary thinks she knows **everything.**

Uncle Don:
I see. Maybe she's just a little too excited about all she's learning at school. She's going to a good school, and I'm glad for her that she's gaining some excellent skills there. She wants to be a teacher, doesn't she?

Jessica:
That's what she says. But she's got some ideas that don't make sense to me.

Uncle Don:
What kind of ideas?

Jessica:
When we were making cookies, Mary started talking to Mom about Jesus. Mary said that Jesus was just a good teacher—He really wasn't God.

Uncle Don:
Jessica, I'm glad you told me about this. I need to sit down with Mary and show her what the Bible says about Jesus.

Jessica:
Mary said that the Bible has some truth in it, but some of it is just stories. Uncle Don, she's gotten me confused. How can we know for sure?

Uncle Don:
Jessica, when we read in the Bible about the Pharisee and the tax collector, we learned that God saw them just the same inside—they were sinners. But only the tax collector saw himself that way. On the outside, the Pharisee pretended to be good, even though he was rotten inside.

Jessica:
That's right.

Uncle Don:
But the Bible is **true, all the way through**. The truth has stood for thousands of years, even though many people have tried to prove it to be false. The Bible is God's Word. **All** of it is true.

Jessica:
Can we know for sure that Jesus is God?

Uncle Don:
Yes, Jessica, we can. The Bible gives us the true story of His life: the miracles He did, the things He said, the fact He never sinned. It shows us that He fulfilled the exact words written about Him hundreds of years before by God's prophets.

Jessica:
There's nobody else like Jesus, is there!

Uncle Don:
No, there isn't, Jessica! Unlike the Pharisee and the tax collector, Jesus Christ is perfect inside as well as outside. He is truly God—as well as being a sinless man and the greatest Teacher.

Jessica:
Mary only had part of the truth, didn't she! Did Jesus' disciples know that He was God?

Uncle Don:
One day Jesus actually showed the "God part" of Himself to some of His disciples. That day, God in Heaven spoke aloud about Jesus, and the disciples heard Him! Let's read that story together!

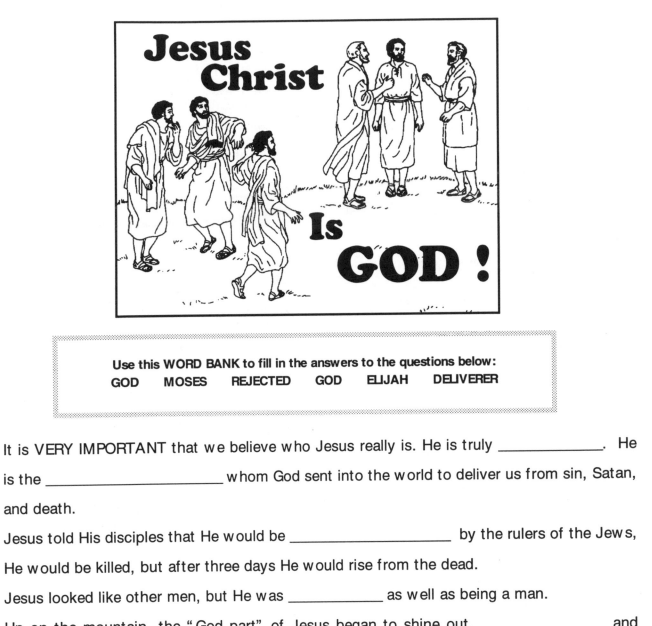

Use this **WORD BANK** to fill in the answers to the questions below:
GOD   MOSES   REJECTED   GOD   ELIJAH   DELIVERER

1. It is VERY IMPORTANT that we believe who Jesus really is. He is truly _____. He is the _____ whom God sent into the world to deliver us from sin, Satan, and death.

2. Jesus told His disciples that He would be _____ by the rulers of the Jews, He would be killed, but after three days He would rise from the dead.

3. Jesus looked like other men, but He was _____ as well as being a man.

4. Up on the mountain, the "God part" of Jesus began to shine out. _____ and _____ appeared there, talking with Jesus.

What did God say about Jesus?

There on the mountain, God spoke about Jesus so the disciples could hear. Look in your Bible in Mark 9:7. Find the words in this verse spoken aloud by God to the disciples. Write these words here: _____

_____

Lesson Scripture: Mark 8:27-31; 9:2-8   **LESSON 42**   Firm **FOUNDATIONS**   **REVIEW SHEET**

Jesus Is the Only Doorway to Eternal Life

Readers: Uncle Don, Travis, Jessica, Jimmy

Uncle Don:
Hi kids! Have you heard about the new park? I understand that Mr. Lewis has hired someone to fix up his old homestead and build some nature trails through his property. It's a beautiful place. I understand he's giving free passes to anyone who asks.

Travis:
We heard about it, all right.

Jessica:
Yeah, and we went. But we couldn't get in!

Uncle Don:
What you mean, "You couldn't get in"?

Jimmy:
I got in! For free! It's **beautiful!**

Travis:
Don't brag about it!

Jimmy:
I'm not bragging.

Uncle Don:
Wait! Tell me about this. Travis, Jessica, why couldn't you get in?

Travis:
It's kind of embarrassing.

Jessica:
We didn't want to have to go see Mr. Lewis, so we decided to get in another way.

Travis:
Some kids I know live up behind Mr. Lewis's property and they said they thought we could just go in under the fence.

Uncle Don:
Travis, that's not right!

Jessica:
That's what I told him! I went with my girls' club. Our leader said she thought the man would let us in because we were a service club. We clean the school playground every Saturday!

Travis:
So what! You didn't get in either!

Uncle Don:
It sounds like neither one of you believed the instructions you were given about getting into the park.

Jessica:
You're right, Uncle Don. I thought for sure the man at the gate would let our club in. Our leader told him all about the things we do to help around town.

Uncle Don:
What did the man say?

Jessica:
He said he really appreciated all the things we did, but Mr. Lewis had left instructions not to let anyone come in without the free pass that Mr. Lewis gives out. I don't think that's fair.

Uncle Don:
Jessica, who does that park belong to?

Jessica:
It belongs to Mr. Lewis.

Uncle Don:
Then Mr. Lewis has the right to say who can come in. He's been very kind and generous to fix it up so people can enjoy it. And he's made a way so anyone can come in.

Travis:
But not under the back fence.

Uncle Don:
I should hope not! What happened, anyway?

Travis:
Well, I went to these boys' house and we walked out back to the fence. We didn't see anyone around. I started to go under the fence and—pow! I really got a shock! I screamed and just then a man came walking up from inside the park.

Uncle Don:
What did he say to you?

Travis:
I was really scared! I thought he'd send me to jail, but he didn't. He told me they had to put the fence up so people wouldn't sneak in. He said that Mr. Lewis wanted the park safe for people to enjoy. He said that all we had to do was to go to Mr. Lewis and he'd give us passes.

Uncle Don:
Jimmy, how did **you** get in? Tell us again.

Jimmy:
I've known Mr. Lewis for a long time. He's really a kind man. He keeps his word. When I heard about the park opening and that he would give passes, I just went to him and asked and he gave me one. Then I went there and the man at the gate looked at my pass and let me in.

Uncle Don:
Kids, I hope you've learned from this. I'd like you to look with me at something in the Bible.

JESUS
is the **only** doorway to eternal life!

Below are six pairs of doors. In each pair, cross out the one that is false. Take the letters under the one that is true and write them in the numbered spaces at the bottom of the page to find the secret message!

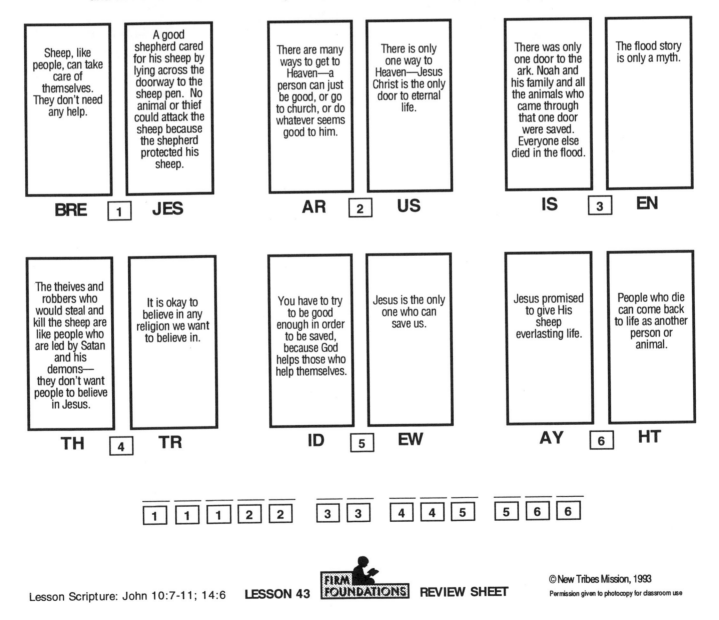

Sheep, like people, can take care of themselves. They don't need any help.	A good shepherd cared for his sheep by lying across the doorway to the sheep pen. No animal or thief could attack the sheep because the shepherd protected his sheep.	There are many ways to get to Heaven—a person can just be good, or go to church, or do whatever seems good to him.	There is only one way to Heaven—Jesus Christ is the only door to eternal life.	There was only one door to the ark. Noah and his family and all the animals who came through that one door were saved. Everyone else died in the flood.	The flood story is only a myth.

BRE [1] JES   AR [2] US   IS [3] EN

The theives and robbers who would steal and kill the sheep are like people who are led by Satan and his demons—they don't want people to believe in Jesus.	It is okay to believe in any religion we want to believe in.	You have to try to be good enough in order to be saved, because God helps those who help themselves.	Jesus is the only one who can save us.	Jesus promised to give His sheep everlasting life.	People who die can come back to life as another person or animal.

TH [4] TR   ID [5] EW   AY [6] HT

[1] [1] [1] [2] [2] [3] [3] [4] [4] [5] [5] [6] [6]

Lesson Scripture: John 10:7-11; 14:6   **LESSON 43**   FIRM FOUNDATIONS   **REVIEW SHEET**

Travis:
Jessica! I can't believe what just happened. We just heard that Mrs. Wilson died!

Jessica:
You're kidding! I thought she just had the flu.

Travis:
That's how it all started. But I guess she had some kind of reaction to some medicine and she died before anyone could get her to the hospital.

Jessica:
I can't believe it. She was so young. She was my teacher last year. I loved her. Now she's dead! I've never had anyone so close to me die.

Uncle Don:
Hi, kids. What's wrong?

Jessica:
Mrs. Wilson, my last year's teacher—she's dead!

Uncle Don:
Oh, Jessica, I'm **so** sorry. I hadn't heard.

Jessica:
I just can't believe it. Friday she was there at school, Monday we heard she was sick, and today—she's dead!

Travis:
Why do people have to die? Why couldn't she have just kept living? She was a nice person.

Jessica:
It's not fair. She shouldn't have died. Why didn't somebody mean die instead?

Uncle Don:
People don't talk very much about death, do they?

Jessica:
No.

Uncle Don:
But in the Bible, God talks a lot about death. Did you ever stop to think—**everyone** eventually dies? Death is the result of sin—**all** people are born sinners, because all people are descendants of Adam, who sinned against God.

Jessica:
I remember studying about that. But it just doesn't seem fair. Mrs. Wilson was so special. Now she's dead, and I'll never see her again.

Uncle Don:
Wait, now, let's think about what God tells us in the Bible. It's true that our bodies all die because of sin. But the Bible tells us that one day, God will give life to all the dead and every person will stand before God. Those who have put their faith in Jesus Christ will live forever with God, but those who have not will spend eternity separated from God.

Jessica:
You mean some people will spend forever in Heaven and some will spend forever in Hell?

Uncle Don:
That's exactly right. I happen to know that Mrs. Wilson is right now with Jesus. She was a sinner, just like the rest of us, but she put her faith in Jesus Christ when she was about your age. I was her Sunday School teacher.

Jessica:
I didn't know that! But I do know that she told us a lot about Jesus.

Uncle Don:
I'll never forget how concerned she was when she realized that she was a sinner, on her way to Hell. When she understood that Jesus Christ had made a way for her to be saved, she immediately put her trust in Him. Her life really changed. Jessica, I will miss her too. But I know I'll see her again—I'll see her in Heaven!

Travis:
I heard one of the men saying that maybe she'd come back here as a bird or a butterfly.

Uncle Don:
Travis, whoever told you that was absolutely wrong. That is a lie of Satan! He wants people to think that there is no penalty for sin—there is no Hell, no judgment—just another life of some kind after this one. When people think that way, they don't see their need of a Saviour.

Jessica:
But why did she have to die now?

Uncle Don:
I don't know. God doesn't tell us everything. But He does tell us in His Word that He made everything and everyone and that He wants everyone to be saved. Our lives really belong to Him. God knows what is the very best, even though we often cannot understand. God has power over life and death. He is the only one who can give life. I'd like to read to you from the Bible about Jesus and a man named Lazarus.

Travis:
Uncle Don, I like Jesus more and more. I don't understand everything, but everything about Jesus is good. I want to hear the story.

Jessica:
Me too. Please read it to us.

Name _____

raised
Lazarus
from the
dead !

Use this word bank to fill in the answers to the following questions. Circle the right answer to the "YES" and "NO" questions.

| loved | God | separated | God | sin | jealous | judged | everything |

1. _____ has the power to give and take life.

2. All people will be raised from the dead and _____ by God.

3. Jesus is _____. He created all things; therefore He is able to give life to the dead.

4. When Jesus said that those who believe in Him will never die, He meant that they will never be _____ from God in the everlasting fire.

5. Was Jesus surprised to find Lazarus dead?   YES   NO

6. Because Jesus is God, He knows _____.

7. Jesus cried because He was sad to see the terrible problems caused by _____ and death, and He cried because He _____ Mary and Martha and their friends and He identified with their grief.

8. The Jewish leaders, the priests and Pharisees and Sadducees, did not like to see the great miracles Jesus performed because they were _____ of Him. They were afraid that the people would try to make Jesus their king. Then the Romans would blame the Jewish leaders and remove them from their important positions.

Lesson Scripture: John 11:1-48   LESSON 44 FIRM FOUNDATIONS REVIEW SHEET

Jesus Loved the Children and Taught the Rich Young Ruler

Readers: Uncle Don, Travis, Jessica

Jessica:
Uncle Don, thank you for taking us to the children's home.

Uncle Don:
You're welcome, Jessica. Thank you for coming with me. What did you think of it?

Travis:
I thought it was kind of sad.

Jessica:
Me too. I didn't realize how many kids were in there. Some of them are so sick.

Travis:
I couldn't believe that one little girl who was paralyzed. She just smiled all the time.

Jessica:
I know it! I'll never forget her! Can we go back and visit her?

Uncle Don:
I'd love to take you!

Travis:
You know, another thing that surprised me was that man that we met there—the guy who talked so much about his money.

Uncle Don:
How did he surprise you, Travis?

Travis:
Well, he just seemed so worried about everything, and he was talking all the time about all the things he had done for the kids.

Uncle Don:
He really has done a lot to help the children. He's a man who has been very generous with his money in a lot of ways. But I know him personally, and he really hasn't put His trust in God. His money is so important to him, and even though he gives a lot, he also keeps a lot for himself. He's always worried about what's happening with his money. I think he's actually trying to buy God's favor with his good deeds.

Jessica:
Maybe it would help him to go to church.

Uncle Don:
There's no doubt it would help him to hear the preaching of God's Word. But this man has gone to church and just considers it something he can do to please God. He needs to see that he is a sinner who can do **nothing** to make himself right with God. All of his good deeds and religious acts will never make him acceptable to God.

Travis:
Uncle Don, have you ever told him that?

Uncle Don:
Yes, I have. He just doesn't want to listen to me or to anything in the Bible. He's a very proud man.

Jessica:
It's kind of strange, but somehow that little girl seems like she's better off than that rich man.

Uncle Don:
Jessica, she really is. But several months ago, she was like a different person. She never smiled.

Travis:
You're kidding!

Uncle Don:
No, it's true. She was bitter about being paralyzed. Nobody could help her. Then a couple of girls came and talked to her. They visited her for several weeks and told her about God.

Jessica:
Kind of like you have told us?

Uncle Don:
Yes. The girls showed her in God's Word that her greatest problem was not her paralysis—it was her sin. When she saw that, she was amazed.

Travis:
I don't think most people would have told her that.

Uncle Don:
No, but it was what she needed to hear. As the girls read the Bible to her and told her about Jesus Christ, that little girl believed! She knew she had nothing to offer God, but she put her faith in Him as her Saviour. She knows now that she has eternal life. She told me, "Jesus has done everything for me! Look, I can't do anything, but God has accepted me because of Jesus."

Jessica:
You know, I felt really sad for her, but now that you have told us, I think I feel lots more sad for that rich man.

Uncle Don:
It really is sad. He's a nice man, but he just isn't willing to believe God's Word. He loves his money more than he loves God, even though he's always doing good deeds. He's like a man Jesus talked to one day. The story is in Mark, chapter 10. Let's look at it together.

Name _____

JESUS
loved the children

and taught the rich young ruler

Answer the questions using this **WORD BANK:**

SIN	MONEY	LOVES	BELIEVE	TEN COMMANDMENTS	BELIEVE	SINNED

1. Jesus _____ children.

2. Children, just like adults, need to be rescued from the power of _____ and Satan and death.

3. God wants us to _____ in His Son, Jesus Christ.

4. The young man who came to Jesus thought He could please God and get into Heaven by obeying the _____ _____ .

5. Jesus wanted this young man to know that only God is good—all men have _____ .

6. The young man went away sad because He refused Jesus and chose to love His _____ more than he loved God.

7. Having a lot of money is not what is important. God tells us that the most important thing in life is to _____ in Jesus Christ.

Lesson Scripture: Mark 10:13-24   **LESSON 45** **FIRM FOUNDATIONS** **REVIEW SHEET**

Uncle Don:
Well, kids, you'll be happy to hear who came to our Bible study last night!

Jessica:
Who was it?

Uncle Don:
Jimmy's Dad, Mr. Johnson!

Travis:
No kidding! That's great!

Uncle Don:
I sure hope it's not too late.

Jessica:
What do you mean?

Uncle Don:
Mr. Johnson just found out that he has a very severe case of lung cancer. The doctors don't give him but a few weeks or months to live.

Travis:
Man, that's gotta be hard for Jimmy.

Uncle Don:
It is. Since Mr. Johnson doesn't have much time left, I've offered to teach them every night for the next several weeks. He's finally seeing that all his money can't buy him anything he needs right now.

Jessica:
What will happen to Jimmy if Mr. Johnson dies?

Uncle Don:
I don't know. His mom lives in another state. We'll just have to see. Right now, things don't look too good for Jimmy.

Travis:
Uncle Don, does it ever seem to you like there's an awful lot of hard things happening?

Uncle Don:
It sure does, Travis. God told us in the Bible that it would be just like this.

Jessica:
It's hard to think about Mr. Johnson. But it's even harder to see kids hurting—like some of the ones we saw in the children's hospital.

Uncle Don:
I know Jessica, I know. One of the hardest things I ever saw was a young girl who got sick while her parents were missionaries in a foreign country. She was sick all the time while she was growing up, and they finally had to come home because she was so sick.

Travis:
What happened to her? Did she get well?

Uncle Don:
No, she just got worse. I've never seen anyone suffer so much. But she was like that little girl we visited—she almost always had a smile. She loved Jesus Christ and had put her trust in Him to save her from her sins and to give her eternal life. She knew she was dying, but she trusted God to take her home to be with Him forever.

Jessica:
Is she still sick?

Uncle Don:
No, she isn't! She finally became so sick that she died. She's with Jesus now!

Jessica:
Uncle Don, I don't like to say this, but it just doesn't seem fair. Her parents were missionaries. Shouldn't God have made her get well?

Uncle Don:
I understand what you mean, Jessica, but I think you need to take a little different look at what happened to her. I sure had to do that. I was thinking just like you are.

Travis:
What do you mean, Uncle Don?

Uncle Don:
Well, it's true that she suffered terribly. But she's in Heaven now, and she will be with God forever. It's just like that little girl in the children's home: life is hard for her, but the hard part is very short compared to eternity.

Jessica:
You're right, Uncle Don. What about Mr. Johnson? I wonder if he's thought about what's going to happen to him when he dies.

Uncle Don:
I hope he's beginning to think about it. The Bible tells us a story about a rich man who refused to think about what would happen when he died. He refused to believe God. And it tells us about a man who, like my friends' daughter, suffered terribly here, but put his faith in God.

Travis
If all these things in the Bible are true, why don't people believe God?

Uncle Don:
That's a good question. God has told us clearly in the Bible what we need to know, but people still refuse to believe.

Name _____

It is FOOLISH to trust in riches!

Find the hidden message! Use the WORD BANK to help you fill in the answers to the questions.

```
            2
            []
        1   []      4           6
        []  []      []      5   []
    T   U   []  I   []  J   S   U
        []  3   []      []
        []  []  []      []
            []  []      []
                []      []
                []
                []
```

WORD BANK:
_____
PUNISHMENT
MOSES
HEAVEN
WORD
LIVES

1. Understanding and believing God's _____ is much more important than being rich!

2. God gave us our _____. He is the one who decides when we will die.

3. The story of the rich man and Lazarus is   TRUE   FALSE .

4. When a person dies, he either goes to Heaven to be with God or to hell, separated from God forever in a place of eternal _____ .

5. After a person dies and goes to hell, he can never leave hell. A person who goes to Heaven will never leave _____ —he will be with God forever!

6. Abraham told the rich man that his brothers must trust in _____ and the prophets, that is, the Old Testament. (Now we have the whole Bible to learn from!)

Lesson Scripture: Luke 12:15-21; 16:19-31

FIRM FOUNDATIONS   LESSON 46   REVIEW SHEET

© New Tribes Mission, 1993
Permission given to photocopy for classroom use

Jimmy:
Uncle Don, I'm still confused about something.

Uncle Don:
What's that, Jimmy?

Jimmy:
Well, I still don't understand about all the lambs and other animals used for sacrifices in the Bible. It just seems kind of cruel.

Uncle Don:
I'm glad you spoke up. It **is** hard to understand, especially since we don't sacrifice animals anymore. There are several things we need to remember.

Jessica:
Like what?

Uncle Don:
Well, the killing of a lamb or other animal was first of all a reminder that **the penalty for sin is death**. Do you remember what happened in the Garden of Eden?

Jessica:
Adam and Eve disobeyed God. Then they hid because they realized they were naked.

Uncle Don:
That's right. And what did God do for them?

Travis:
He made them clothes out of animal skins.

Uncle Don:
Yes, God killed animals to clothe Adam and Eve. Before they sinned, there was no death. But because they sinned, death came into the world. The Bible says that **without the shedding of blood, sin cannot be paid for**.

Jimmy:
Adam and Eve really should have been the ones to die—not the animals!

Uncle Don:
That's exactly right! But because of God's mercy and grace, He made coverings for them—**He was the only one who could make them acceptable to Him.**

Jessica:
They tried to cover themselves up with leaves.

Uncle Don:
Yes, but God wouldn't accept those clothes they made—He won't accept anything we try to do to make ourselves acceptable to God. That's another reason for the sacrifice. It is **GOD'S WAY for us to come to Him—by FAITH.**

Travis:
Abel came God's way, but Cain didn't.

Jessica:
Abel brought an animal from his flock.

Uncle Don:
And he was accepted by God because he came **believing God**, agreeing with God about his sin. Do you remember the Passover?

Travis:
God told the Israelites to kill a perfect lamb for each family.

Jessica:
When God saw the blood, He passed over them!

Uncle Don:
Exactly. The lamb also reminds us of **the separation between God and man**. In the days of the tabernacle and temple, the High Priest was the only one who could enter into the holy of holies. He had to bring the blood of a lamb and sprinkle it on the mercy seat.

Jessica:
But it didn't really pay for their sins.

Uncle Don:
No, God had something better planned. For thousands of years people had brought lambs to God. All of those who came **by faith** would be included in what God planned to do. He made a promise, clear back in the Garden.

Jimmy:
To send the Deliverer?

Uncle Don:
Yes! Listen: In Abel's day, God required that a lamb be killed **for each man's sins**. Then, at the first Passover, God also required **a lamb for each family**.

Travis:
And later on, the high priest brought a lamb **for the whole nation**!

Uncle Don:
But do you remember what John the Baptist said about Jesus Christ?

Jimmy:
He called Him the **Lamb of God who takes away the sins of the whole world!**

Uncle Don:
Jesus was going to celebrate the Passover with His disciples. It would be the final Passover celebration in God's eyes. But this time, the lamb to be offered was Jesus Himself!

Jesus entered Jerusalem and was betrayed by Judas

JESUS gave the Lord's Supper

WORD BANK: BLOOD   SAVE   GOD   BODY   SINFULNESS   SINNERS

1. Jesus refused the people's offer for Him to be their king. He knew that they just wanted someone to deliver them from the Roman government. They didn't realize that they were sinners who needed Jesus to _____ them from Satan, sin, and death.

2. Judas had been one of Jesus' disciples, but he had never realized his own _____ . He never put his trust in Jesus as His Saviour.

3. Jesus knew what Judas planned to do because Jesus is _____ . He knows everything.

4. Jesus said that the broken bread was like His own _____ .

5. Jesus said that the wine was like His own _____, which would soon flow out of His body for _____ .

Lesson Scripture: Mark 11:1-10;
14:1,2,10-26

LESSON 47 FIRM FOUNDATIONS **REVIEW SHEET**

Jesus Was Arrested by His Enemies

Readers: Uncle Don, Travis, Jessica, Jimmy

Jimmy:
Uncle Don, I just can't understand why people didn't like Jesus.

Uncle Don:
It really is hard to understand. But people back in those days were a lot like people now.

Jessica:
How do you mean, Uncle Don?

Uncle Don:
Many people today are just like the Pharisees and the other officials who hated Jesus. Though they might not realize it, they are under Satan's leadership; they are against God. The Pharisees and religious leaders who were trying to kill Jesus were jealous of Him.

Travis:
But Jesus did so many good things! They should have loved Him! He never did anything wrong!

Uncle Don:
You are absolutely right—but that's what made them so jealous. Many of the people followed Jesus. They even wanted to make Him king. He really was their rightful king—He was a descendant of King David, and the throne was rightfully His, both in the line of David and as the great King of Kings—God Himself!

Jessica:
Didn't the Pharisees understand that?

Uncle Don:
They saw His miracles, and they saw that He was very popular with the people. They were afraid for their own positions of rulership. Besides, Jesus told the truth about them—that they were really sinners. So they were jealous of Him and they hated Him for telling the truth.

Jimmy:
But since Jesus was really God, couldn't He have kept them from doing anything bad to Him?

Uncle Don:
Yes, Jimmy, He certainly could have. The Bible tells us that Jesus could have called thousands of angels to help Him.

Travis:
Why didn't He?

Uncle Don:
Jesus knew that He **must** die. That was God's great plan to deliver people from sin and Satan and death. He knew exactly what He was going to have to go through—every detail was written down hundreds of years before by God's prophets.

Jimmy:
So He knew all that, even before He came to earth as a man?

Uncle Don:
Yes, Jimmy, He knew, and He wanted to do it—for us.

Travis:
That's incredible!

Jessica:
Couldn't He have done it some easier way?

Uncle Don:
No, Jessica, His death was the only thing that would completely pay for sins. God wouldn't accept anything else.

Travis:
I can't understand how He could do it—knowing what was going to happen.

Uncle Don:
He really suffered when He faced the things that He knew were going to happen. Jesus was going to take the full punishment for the sins of every person that ever lived. Remember, sin separates us from God. Jesus was ready to accept all of that for us. But you're right. It was a terrible thing to face.

Jimmy:
So you're saying that Jesus knew everything that was going to happen to Him; He had the power to stop it; but He was going to take it anyway, **for us**?

Uncle Don:
Yes, Jimmy. That's exactly right.

Jessica:
It's just not fair. He didn't deserve all that!

Uncle Don:
No, He didn't, but we do, and He was going to do it for us.

Travis:
Did Jesus know that we would be alive now?

Uncle Don:
Yes, Travis, He did.

Jimmy:
So all the things that happened to Him should have happened to us instead!

Uncle Don:
Yes, Jimmy—Jesus took all the punishment for us, and for all the people of the whole world.

JESUS was arrested by His enemies

Use this WORD BANK to fill in the answers:
holy   prayed   nothing   Satan   thorns

1. Jesus _____ in the garden. He was going to face the most terrible suffering any man has ever faced.

2. _____ was leading Judas and the Jewish leaders to arrest and kill Jesus.

3. Jesus had never done anything wrong. He was _____ and perfect. He did not deserve to die. When false witnesses spoke against Him, He said _____ .

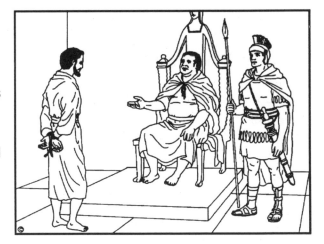

4. God's prophets had told years before what was going to happen to Jesus. Everything they said about Him came true. Jesus had a purple robe put on Him, a crown of _____ was put on His head, and He was beaten and made fun of.

Jessica:
Uncle Don, can you tell us more about what happened to Jesus? I thought I understood, but it all seems so much more terrible now that we are reading it from the Bible. They were so mean to Him!

Uncle Don:
It was terrible, Jessica. Jesus was suffering the punishment for all the sins of every person who ever lived.

Jessica:
And He'd never done anything wrong!

Uncle Don:
No, He hadn't, and He was completely willing to suffer it all. Everything in the Bible pointed to this one thing: Jesus was going to die for sinners.

Travis:
Did the people know what was happening?

Uncle Don:
Not really. Even Jesus' disciples were confused. They thought that Jesus was going to be their King and deliver them from the Roman rule. But now they were watching Him be crucified.

Jimmy:
What does "crucified" mean?

Uncle Don:
It means that He was nailed to a wooden Cross and left there to die. To put a person to death this way was probably the most cruel form of the death penalty. Today we use the electric chair, and a person dies almost instantly. But a person who was crucified might hang there on the Cross for days before he would die. It was just terrible suffering.

Travis:
I keep thinking, He could have escaped all that! But He didn't! He really wanted to do it, for us.

Jessica:
He was already beaten and then they'd flogged Him, too.

Jimmy:
And they put that awful crown of thorns on His head, and they spit on Him.

Uncle Don:
But He never once defended Himself—He just took it all quietly. He was hanging there on the Cross, between two men who deserved to die. It's hard to imagine how much He was suffering.

Travis:
It just seems so awful. Why couldn't God have made another way?

Uncle Don:
Sin separates us from God. The penalty for sin is death. God could never forgive our sins unless the punishment for our sins was completely paid. Jesus paid that price for us by suffering death in our place.

Jimmy:
But He'd never sinned!

Uncle Don:
No, and that was why God could accept His death for us. Do you remember the animals that were brought for sacrifice? They had to be perfect.

Travis:
Like the ram that was caught in the bush by the horns—the one that God provided for Isaac?

Uncle Don:
Exactly. Nothing but a perfect sacrifice would do. We could never pay the price for our sins. Only Jesus could do it.

Jessica:
Did He really take all of our sins to the Cross with Him? Everything? Even the horrible things people do, like murder?

Uncle Don:
Yes, Jessica, even murder. Even the little things that we try to forget—those sins still are sin and had to be paid for in full on the Cross. Every little lie, every unkind word, every act of disobedience, every bad attitude.

Jessica:
Oh, Uncle Don, Jesus did that for me! He did that for **my** sins!

Uncle Don:
Yes, Jessica, for you! He became, for a time, completely separated from God the Father. When Jesus took our sins on Himself at the Cross, God could not have fellowship with Him. Just as our sins separate us from God, our sins separated Jesus from His Father at that terrible time.

Jessica:
He took my punishment! He died for me!

Uncle Don:
Yes, Jessica! He did absolutely everything that was needed to pay the punishment for your sins and for the sins of everyone in the whole world! Oh, I'm so glad you believe!

JESUS
was crucified and buried

WORD BANK: OUR SEPARATED SATISFIED SINS PUNISHMENT BLOOD

1. Jesus was crucified so He could die to pay for the _____ of the whole world.

2. While Jesus was on the cross, there were three hours of darkness. This was God's sign that Jesus was taking the punishment for sin by being _____ from God.

3. When Jesus said, "It is finished," He meant that He had finished the work of bearing the complete _____ for sin so that people could be delivered from the power of Satan, sin, and death.

4. Jesus had never sinned; He was dying for _____ sins.

5. God ripped the temple curtain from top to bottom to show that He was fully _____ with the payment Jesus had made for sin. God was showing that there was no more need for the _____ of animals in the most holy place.

Lesson Scripture: Mark 15:20-46   **LESSON 49** FIRM FOUNDATIONS **REVIEW SHEET**

The Meaning of Christ's Death

Readers: Uncle Don, Travis, Jessica

Travis:
Uncle Don, how can a person be saved?

Uncle Don:
There's only one way, Travis: a person must admit that he is a sinner, unable to save himself, and he must put his faith in what Jesus did for him when He died on the Cross.

Travis:
You mean that's all there is to it?

Uncle Don:
There was a lot to it for Jesus; but for us, we must simply accept what He did for us by dying in our place.

Jessica:
I have accepted His payment for me!

Uncle Don:
Jessica, I'm so thankful that you have! God wants **everyone** to put their faith in Him!

Travis:
Does God really want **everybody**?

Uncle Don:
The Bible tells us that God loved the whole world so much that He sent Jesus Christ to die for every person's sins. The Bible also says that God is not willing for any person to perish; He wants every person to be saved.

Travis:
It's hard to imagine God really wanting everyone.

Uncle Don:
That shows how great His love is! Remember, Travis, it was **God** who **created man**. Do you remember how the Bible tells in Genesis about the friendship God had with Adam in the garden before Adam and Eve sinned?

Jessica:
God actually walked and talked with Adam!

Uncle Don:
That's right, Jessica. God created man and loved man and made man in God's own image. God made man to have friendship with God.

Travis:
I wish it was like that now.

Uncle Don:
When Adam and Eve sinned, that wonderful friendship was broken. Man was separated from God, and there was nothing man could do to get back to God. Instead of eternal life with God, man faced death and eternity in Hell.

Travis:
Don't people know that now? Don't people know that they are going to Hell?

Uncle Don:
They should. God has made it very clear in His Word. But He has also made very clear the way back to Him—the Bible points us to Jesus Christ.

Jessica:
You mean, kind of like a signpost?

Uncle Don:
Yes, Jessica. All through the Old Testament God gave us directions, descriptions, and pointers to show us the way to Himself. Every one of these was pointing toward the Deliverer, Jesus Christ.

Travis:
How can people miss the way?

Uncle Don:
Many people never read the Bible. Some people never seem to be concerned about God or the Bible. They don't think they need God. Other people think that God is there, but they think they have to **do** something to make themselves acceptable to Him.

Jessica:
They wouldn't think that way if they read the "road signs," would they!

Uncle Don:
You are absolutely right! God has made His Word very clear. Jesus Christ is the only way back to God. God will accept only those people who come to Him trusting in Jesus because of what He did on the Cross to pay for sin.

Travis:
Do you mean that God wants me just to trust in Jesus who died for my sins? Will God really accept me if I put my trust in His Son who died for me? I don't even have to do anything?

Jessica:
Travis, Uncle Don has been telling us that for a long time!

Travis:
I know, but now I see what he means. It's so simple. **Jesus died for me!** God accepts me because of what Jesus did for me on the Cross!

Uncle Don:
Travis! You do believe! And it's just like Jesus told Nicodemus—believing is really a new birth. Welcome to God's family!

Jessica:
Now we're brother and sister in God's family, too!

Name _____

JESUS
Rose from the Dead, Appeared to His Disciples, and Ascended into Heaven!

WORD BANK: Jesus   judge   stone   Son of God   sinners   body   earthquake

1. When the women went to the tomb where Jesus had been buried, they found that the _____ had been rolled away from the entrance to the tomb.

2. Before the women arrived at the tomb, there had been a great _____, and God had sent His angel to roll the stone away from the entrance.

3. When the women entered the tomb they saw two angels, but they did not see the _____ of Jesus.

4. Jesus' resurrection shows us that He was truly the _____ ____ _____. He truly was the Deliverer, just as He had claimed to be. God accepted Him fully.

5. We can be forgiven by God and receive the gift of everlasting life by agreeing with God that we are helpless _____ and by trusting only in _____ , who died on the cross for our sins and who rose from the dead to give us eternal life.

6. Jesus will come back to this earth one day to _____ all who refuse to believe in Him. All of those people who do not believe in Jesus Christ will be thrown into the Lake of Fire with Satan and his demons.

Lesson Scripture: Mark 14:61,62;
Luke 24:1-32,35-48; Acts 1:9-11

LESSON 50   FIRM FOUNDATIONS   REVIEW SHEET

© New Tribes Mission, 1993
Permission given to photocopy for classroom use

Jessica:
Uncle Don, where's Jimmy? He never misses our Bible study.

Uncle Don:
Jimmy and his dad are getting ready to go and visit Jimmy's mom. Mrs. Johnson hasn't seen her husband nor Jimmy for a couple of years.

Travis:
Does she know that Mr. Johnson has cancer?

Uncle Don:
Yes, she does. He called her last night, after he put his trust in Jesus Christ as his Saviour!

Jessica and Travis (together):
Mr. Johnson got saved?!

Uncle Don:
Yes! I wish you could have seen and heard him. He looks and talks like a new man. And Jimmy is **so** happy.

Travis:
What about Jimmy? Does he understand that Jesus died for his sins?

Uncle Don:
Yes, he said he put his faith in Jesus a couple of weeks ago.

Jessica:
I thought so! He learned everything so fast. It was kind of like he believed everything we read in the Bible right away.

Uncle Don:
Jimmy has been through a lot of sadness and hurting—he was really glad to hear the Good News about Jesus.

Jessica:
What about Jimmy's older brother, Eddie? Isn't he still in some place where they're trying to keep him off drugs?

Uncle Don:
Yes. Mr. Johnson wants to visit Eddie on the way back here. He is so eager to begin to teach Eddie about God's plan of salvation. Seeing the change God has made in Mr. Johnson's life may make Eddie want to learn about God.

Travis:
Uncle Don, everything you've told us about God is true—but God is even better than I thought. He's wonderful! **Nothing** is too hard for Him!

Jessica:
You're right, Travis! Look at all the things God is doing! I'm so glad about Mr. Johnson! It's still sad that he has cancer, but now, well, even if he dies from it like the doctors said, we'll still see him again in Heaven. Mr. Johnson is **forgiven**, and so are we!

Uncle Don:
Jessica, that's what makes Jesus so special. A lot of religions claim to help people. But there is no one else who offers complete forgiveness for sins and eternal life with the Living God. Jesus alone died for our sins, was buried, and rose again on the third day!

Travis:
It's hard to imagine! He actually took all our sins on Him at the cross. And he died. But tell us again, Uncle Don, what happened then?

Uncle Don:
This is one of the greatest parts of the story! Jesus was buried in a tomb. But after three days, God raised Him back to life!

Jessica:
Did people see him alive?

Uncle Don:
They certainly did! His disciples saw Him, and the Bible tells us in I Corinthians that over 500 people saw Him at one time!

Travis:
I'd sure like to have been there then!

Jessica:
Me too!

Uncle Don:
Me too! **We will see Him** one day, because He is still alive in Heaven. And He is coming back to earth again one day, but this time not to bring salvation. He's already finished that job.

Jessica:
Why is He coming?

Uncle Don:
He is coming again to judge all those who have not believed in Him.

Travis:
When is He coming?

Uncle Don:
The Bible doesn't tell us. But believers are told to go and tell everyone in the world about Him!

Jessica:
Uncle Don, I want to tell everybody I know about Jesus.

Travis:
Me too! I want all my friends to know Him!

But God sent
Jesus Christ
to die
for our sins!

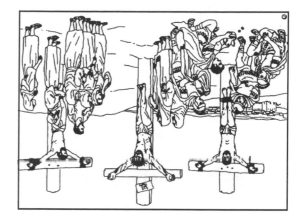

"... while we were yet sinners,
Christ died for us."
Romans 5:8

Jesus had
never sinned,
and God accepted
His death
in place of ours
as full payment
for our sins.

God "made him to be sin for us,
who knew no sin;
that we might be made the
righteousness of God in him."
II Corinthians 5:21

Jesus died
for our sins,
He was buried,
and
He rose again
on the third day!

I Corinthians 15:3-8

God
loves

If you have realized that
you are a sinner
and you believe that
Jesus died for your sins,
then you may like
to thank God
at this time
for giving Jesus
as
your Saviour!

He appeared to His disciples and to many others before He went back to Heaven.

There is nothing we can do to pay for our sins.

"... the wages of sin is death...."
Romans 6:23

The penalty for sin is death.

He is perfect, without sin.

God is holy—

"... your iniquities have separated between you and your God, and your sins have hid his face from you...."
Isaiah 59:2

Sin separates us from God.

But the Bible tells us that **everyone** has sinned.

"...for all have sinned...."
Romans 3:23

The Bible tells us that if you believe that Jesus died for your sins, God will forgive your sins and give you eternal life!

"For God so loved the world, that he gave his only begotten Son, that whosoever believeth in him should not perish, but have everlasting life."
John 3:16

There is no other way to be saved.

"Jesus saith unto him, I am the way, the truth, and the life: no man cometh unto the Father, but by me. "
John 14:6

"Neither is there salvation in any other: for there is none other name under heaven given among men, whereby we must be saved."
Acts 4:12